TORI AM...

ALL THESE YEARS

BY KALEN ROGERS

Thanks to Tori; John Witherspoon; all at Atlantic, East West, and Spivak Entertainment; and Rup.

Special thanks to Dr. Edison and Mary Ellen Amos for their invaluable assistance.

UK ISBN 0.7119.4827.5
US ISBN 0.8256.1448.1
Order No. OP 47756

EXCLUSIVE DISTRIBUTORS
Book Sales Limited
8/9 Frith Street, London W1V 5TZ, UK

Music Sales Corporation
257 Park Avenue South, New York, NY 10010 USA

Music Sales Pty. Limited
120 Rothschild Street, Rosebery, Sydney, NSW 2018, Australia

PHOTO CREDITS
Nancy Bennett
pages 112, 126, 131
Michael Friel
pages 76, 117, 118, 120, 122
Melody McDaniel
pages 28, 82
Cindy Palmano
pages 2, 54, 64, 68, 70, 78 (top), 86, 88, 90, 98, 102, 106, 116, 127
Alan Friedman
pages 110 (three on left), 124
Ramkin
Back cover, pages 108, 110 (right), 114,
Aaron Rappaport
page 36 (bottom right)
Billy Reckert
pages 18 (top left, bottom right), 22 (top left, top right), 26, 58, 94
Eric Rosse
pages 48 (middle & bottom left, right), 50, 60 (top), 62, 74 (three on right), 78 (bottom), 80
Helmut Werb/Retna Ltd.
Front cover, page 132

Color separations by Color 4 Graphics, Milwaukee, Wisconsin
Printed and bound in the United States of America by
Vicks Lithograph and Printing Corporation

LONDON/NEW YORK/PARIS/SYDNEY

INTRODUCTION

Tori Amos has brought the piano back to life. She has taken an instrument too often associated with long-dead composers, frowning pupils, near-sighted teachers, and "Chopsticks," set it in the middle of a stage and played it within an inch of its life. Through Tori, the piano has become the weapon of power and passion that the electric guitar was for a previous generation.

She has rediscovered her own inner voice, and through her unsettlingly honest music has taken us with her on an arduous journey. Her songs are at once sympathetic and exhilarating, offering solace while demanding that we face our demons.

Musically, she has proven that a classically trained child prodigy can combine the madness of Béla Bartók, a smattering of Beatles-inspired songwriting, and some bitchin' Led Zeppelin to create a style all her own.

Armed with the knowledge that "the Ladies' Room is a secret society, and when those lipsticks come out it's the heaviest artillery in the world—the guys have no idea what they're in for," she has taught us more about ourselves than we wanted to know.

Her albums *Little Earthquakes, Under the Pink,* and *Boys For Pele* have reached a diverse collection of humanity who have responded to the many inherent personalities contained in her songs with joyful recognition. Music that can reach right in and rip out your innermost feelings of guilt, oppression, and confusion and give you in return a sense of hope is hard to come by. Tori has the capacity to bring out in the spotlight what most people keep locked in their cellars, zap it with a magic wand, and turn it into something beautiful.

PAST LIVES AND PIANOS

(? ? ? ? — 1 9 6 8)

There is more than one Tori Amos. The carefree little girl, the Tart, the provocative performer, the pixie, the poet, the minister's daughter—all of these personas belong to Tori and none of them begin to describe her. She often alludes to the many facets of her own personality, referring to different aspects of herself as "she" and "the girl," saying, "You can compartmentalize different sides of yourself. You put them onto different shelves, and then bring them out when you need them. Everybody has a barroom personality and a Sunday-lunch personality; they have one personality with their husband and a different personality for their tennis instructor."

She firmly believes in reincarnation and will blithely recite the many people she has been through the 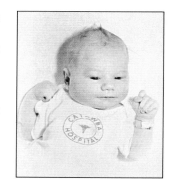 ages, protesting, "of course I believe in having past lives, I mean, three-quarters of the human race believes this, it's not like a great new thought here." After discussing her theory that "there's a part of me that's Sven the Viking, and if anybody tries to hurt that girl again, he'll annihilate them" with a journalist the resulting quote "became a snowball that just wouldn't stop… I mean now I get Viking hats before shows." The disparate nature of Tori's documented bloodline is almost as fascinating as her assortment of past lives. Her mother's side of the family boasts an abundance of full-blooded Cherokee Indians, and Tori delights in telling of her great-great-grandmother Margaret Little, one of the rare refugees left in the Smoky Mountains after the exodus of the 1836 Trail of Tears. According to family legend, Tori's precursor "expressed herself by splitting doorsteps in two with her tomahawk when riled." The other side of Tori's ancestry stems from France and from Scots who sailed over to America to stake their claim on the Native American soil, and includes two great-grandfathers who fought in the Civil War in the Confederate Army. With such a paradoxical heritage, it's no wonder Tori finds warring factions within her own character.

The eclectic mix of familial influences in Tori's life was not confined to interesting ancestors. Her father, Dr. Edison Amos, is a Methodist minister who had studied pre-med in preparation for his original plan to become a physician. His wife Mary Ellen is a Southern belle with a fondness for Nat King Cole who inherited her Cherokee ancestors' gift for frighteningly accurate premonitions and dream interpretation. In 1962 they were a young couple with two children, nine-year-old Mike and seven-year-old Marie, living in a church parsonage in the Washington, D.C., suburb of Georgetown. Caught up in the optimism surrounding John F. Kennedy's presidential election at the end of the year, they decided to have another child. Tori begs to differ, stating that it was *she* who chose to become a member of the Amos family.

While her parents were visiting Tori's grandparents-to-be, a doctor grounded the very pregnant Mary Ellen, forbidding her to return home. Tori was supposed to be born at the Georgetown Hospital in Washington, D.C., but adhering to someone else's plan has never been her strong point. After all, her grandparents' home was to be the backdrop for many a happy childhood summer; Tori simply decided to spend summer number one there as well. She picked the place, but her parents picked the name, and so Tori was born Myra Ellen Amos on August 22, 1963, at the Old Catawba Hospital in Newton, North Carolina.

In her two sets of grandparents Tori experienced two very contradictory sets of influences. Her mother's parents taught her about nature, dreams, and alternative medicine. Tori and her grandfather "Poppa" spent many a sympathetic hour together as he taught her Cherokee legends and beliefs. Renowned for his singing voice and perfect pitch, he sang to Tori from the day she was born. Her father's

Bertie Marie Akins Copeland (Nannie) and Calvin Clinton Copeland

James W. Amos (Grandfather)

Addie Allen Amos ('Victorian' Grandmother)

side of the family tree furnished her with a perhaps more conventional if more stringent set of grandparents in James and Addie Allen Amos, both well-educated ordained ministers. The couple moved from their post as missionaries in the Appalachian mountains in Virginia to Baltimore during World War II to join in the war effort. The catalyst for much guilt, shame, and confusion later to be exorcised in song, Grandma Amos's rigid morality contrasted sharply with the value system Tori was learning from her Cherokee grandparents.

Tori's "Victorian" grandmother has since had bestowed upon her by her granddaughter the notorious title of "the female St. Paul of this century" who "believed in virgins forever. My grandmother revered St. Paul; funny, he took sensuality and sexuality out of the goddess and basically circumcised passion out of the female role model, the Mother Mary. Consequently, Christian women have been divided for 2,000 years." Grandma Amos has become infamous through Tori's description to audiences around the world of the castigating letters her grandmother used to pen detailing the sins of premarital sex and the evils of passion.

At the ripe old age of two and a half, Tori Amos found her calling in the living room of her family's new home in Baltimore, Maryland. While her older brother and sister were dutifully practicing for their obligatory piano lessons, little Tori was listening, and when they'd had their turn on the piano stool, she would toddle up and tickle the ivories herself. Soon she was playing classical pieces, popular tunes, and anything else that caught her ear. The Amos's piano, along with Nannie's organ in North Carolina, became additional members of Tori's family. She remembers "this huge black upright. It had one of those winding stools on it that could wind down low or wind up really high, and I would wind it down to get on it and then I would ask my brother to wind it up so I could reach the keys. He would always wind it up for me."

At Nannie's organ (age 2)

A deceptively demure Tori at the Amos piano

Chatting with Nannie

A future in music wasn't all that began to show itself in young Tori. As social as they came, she delighted in carrying on animated conversations on a variety of decidedly unusual topics with all and sundry. Tori's adult reputation as a fascinating if sometimes baffling interviewee was developed and finely honed through years of practice. Intermeshing *tête-à-têtes* with the little wooden people atop the piano, her grandmother, and various composers all before breakfast was no problem for the talkative three-year-old. A history of theological debates with her father began at an early age; Dr. Amos recalls, "the first time I told Tori the Christmas story, she asked me what would have happened if Joseph had emerged from the manger shouting 'Wow! It's a girl!'"

THE PEABODY YEARS

(1968 — 1974)

The fact that their daughter was composing tunes before she could string together a full sentence and could play anything she took a fancy to after hearing it once convinced the Amoses that they had something of a prodigy on their hands. At the age of five Tori was outfitted in a tiny blue dress made for her by one of the doting old women in the church and escorted to Baltimore's Peabody Conservatory of Music for an audition. "I remember everything about it," she asserts. "I remember these people sitting there, and I was an object to them, and I was aware of that. I could do things. I Seuss character." impressive her acceptance on a was the youngest tigious institute  I was a *thing* that felt a bit like a Dr. Nonetheless, her performance led to full scholarship; she student the pres- had ever admitted.

Herein began a six-year roller-coaster ride of inspiration and stifled creativity, joy and frustration, intense happiness and intense failure. Tori attended classes at the Peabody every Saturday, and began to live for the weekends before most children her age knew what day it was. The Peabody was a haven, a place filled with and devoted to music; perhaps more importantly, a place filled with other students who loved music. Tori's varied group of friends, imaginary and real, suddenly expanded tenfold. The other students welcomed the young talent to their world, and treated her as an equal. She lived vicariously through the sixties with her older friends, absorbing everything from their trendy bell-bottoms to their concerns about the Vietnam War. Perhaps most paramount was her exposure to their music; classical music may have been the reason they were all there, but it wasn't all they were about, and Tori fell in love with the sound of the Beatles, Led Zeppelin, and Jimi Hendrix as quickly and as fully as she had with that of Mozart, Beethoven, and Bartók.

However, the overriding delight of playing the piano was, for Tori, being systematically squelched. In order to "break her ear," she was to be taught to read music, beginning with the rather less-than-infectious "Hot Cross Buns." It was a shock to the system, and one which Tori responded to with characteristic defiance. Begging—and oftentimes attempting to bribe—her brother and sister to play the pieces she was meant to sightread just once so that she could pick them up by ear often led to a furious and frustrated Tori. Her penchant for "conversation" with late great composers, consisting of the little pianist playing a variation on one of the master's pieces and then enquiring if he had liked what she'd done, was considered inappropriate, if not blasphemous, by the professors at Peabody. "There was a way to play the classics, and if you deviated from a professor's interpretation, you wouldn't win the competition."

Meanwhile, there were six other days in the week, and Tori's varied lifestyle didn't stop at Peabody. Alternately everyone's favorite "sweetpea" at the Epworth Chapel Methodist Church on Sundays and just one of many children new to the public school system Monday through Friday, Tori found herself in a different world at every turn. "Kindergarten went O.K.," she recalls. "The first grade was fair. The second grade was a bummer. I sat in the corner more than any other kid in the class until the ninth grade. I tried to be an inspiring force, but my teachers and I were at odds. Independent thinking was not their priority." She tolerated life most of the year, and spent summers with Nannie and Poppa in North Carolina, "the magical kingdom."

In June of 1972 Reverend Amos moved his family to Silver Spring, Maryland, where he was the pastor of a new church, the Good Shepherd United Methodist.

A duet with Nanny (age 7)

Stylish at age 9—note the early penchant for rebellious shoes

Mrs. Amos, Tori, sister Marie, brother Mike, Dr. Amos, and a distinctly clerical cake

Tori was almost nine years old now, and found that she had left the sweet old ladies of her former church far behind. She was no longer greeted with adoration each Sunday, but rather was subjected to relentless criticism by several "old bitches" who singled out the minister's daughter as their prey. "If her skirt wasn't too short, it was too long," remembers Tori's mother. "She would come home from church each week and go to her room and cry. She wanted to run away with Robert Plant, firmly arguing that he would understand, and that they would inspire each other"—a prediction that twenty years later would become a truth. School in the new town was a means to an end. "I only went to keep my mother from being arrested." She now had to commute to Peabody on Saturdays, with her father driving and waiting in Baltimore all day for her to finish; she also took additional repertoire classes at the home of her teacher Paula Gorelkin. An audition at Peabody each year was necessary to continue her scholarship, and Tori was constantly being graded and judged on her playing. She was awarded many trophies and honors during these years; a certificate presented by the American College of Musicians U.S.A. has as its curious motto, "Piano-playing is an ideal, all-weather, lifetime hobby or a profitable profession." A 1973 piano teacher's report card notes that "you have much enthusiasm to put into your music… try hard to listen to every sound you make—does it match your image?" along with the encouraging remark "Good for you—you really tried to sing!"

Tori's mischievous side had not disappeared; she says, "I remember liking this boy. He was from the ghetto, and he was there on a scholarship. He could sing this soul, this blue-eyed soul, and I would sit and listen to him. And I wanted to go run away with him, but my father wasn't open to that."

Fifth grade was an interesting year. "I got my period; I smoked my first joint." The piano remained her first and best friend, however, and she loyally rushed home from school each day to sit at the piano bench. Tori's mother waited for her at the bus stop every afternoon, and Tori often begged off an invitation to hang out at a friend's house by using her mother as an excuse; she admits now that she just wanted to get home to her music although leafing through *Playgirl* magazines with Connie and Emily was tempting.

In January of 1973, her Cherokee grandfather Poppa Copeland died, and Tori was devastated. In tribute to this very prominent influence in her life the ten-year-old played and sang his favorite hymns at the funeral in North Carolina. Mrs. Amos believes, "she never got over his death. He was the only person she ever completely respected. She would go to his grave three times a week and sing to him until she was thirteen."

In December of that year Tori's "Victorian" grandmother died, and a mere five months later, the Amos family returned to North Carolina for yet another funeral as an uncle had died suddenly at the age of fifty-seven. They returned to Silver Spring for Tori's annual Peabody audition, at which she played the required and prepared pieces in her own inimitable style. A few

days later Dr. and Mrs. Amos were informed that their daughter's full scholarship had not been renewed, which, according to Tori, "was an out for the Peabody of course. We were poor. They knew that. No scholarship meant no school, so it was a chicken-shit way out." Tori was torn between two conflicting reactions. "I think I was feeling my father's need for me to stay in school, and that freaked me out, that made me feel like I'd failed. But there was a sense of relief, like, finally I can go make some real music. That was a part of me, but the other part was, I was eleven and I was trying to please my father. He wanted me to get my doctorate from the Peabody by the time I was eighteen."

"CAN'T STOP
WHAT IS ON ITS WAY"

(1974—1984)

The following year brought even more change to Tori's life. Her brother Mike, her main musical collaborator, was married in July; in September her sister Marie went away to college in Virginia. The gaping hole created by the loss of the music and the people of the Peabody Institute seemed even darker and larger having to face the fact that she hadn't become the concert pianist everyone had predicted she would become. In a sense, the child prodigy had become the prodigy who failed at eleven years old. Adolescence, which Tori has since described as "the cruelest place on earth," was proving to be quite a trial. At the age of twelve Tori wrote a song entitled "More Than Just a Friend" for a boy on whom she had a tremendous crush, and played the song at a school assembly despite the boy's threat to beat her up if she went ahead with it. She went ahead with it. They never spoke again, but he did not, in the end, beat her up.

Although over a year passed, Tori did not show signs of picking herself up and being the creative force she always had been, and in fact seemed to be sinking deeper into a depression that did not allow her to touch the piano. Hoping to motivate his daughter and bring her back to her music, her father suggested that she reaudition for the Peabody scholarship. Preparing for the audition got Tori's blood flowing again, but the devil in her prevailed, and once faced with the Peabody board she launched into an all-too-appropriate rendition of "I've Been Cheated." She was not readmitted.

At the urging of Tori's parents and at least one dismayed Peabody professor, Patricia Springer, who insisted on continuing to teach Tori privately, Tori and the piano persevered. Now that the hitherto planned career as a concert pianist seemed in Tori's mind's eye to be out the window, she bulldozed ahead with her

School photo, age 13

Everybody else's girl

"I always thought I'd make a good girlfriend for Jesus"

scheme to become a "rock star," a goal which hadn't been far from her mind ever since the first time she heard the Beatles belt out "Sgt. Pepper's." Singing in the church choir and performing in school musicals wasn't quite high-profile enough for Tori, and in March of 1977 she decided to enter the county Teen Talent Contest. With a first-place trophy, her picture in the newspaper, and $100 in prize money under her belt, she was ready to rock and roll.

With the clairvoyant burst of understanding of "you either support your kid or you lose your kid" and a healthy dose of the old "if you can't beat 'em, join 'em" attitude, Tori's father came up with a way for her to further her career and put the Peabody chapter behind her. To the amazement of his thirteen-year-old daughter, Reverend Amos suggested that she get a job playing the piano. At the beginning of the summer of 1977, Tori and Dr. Amos descended upon the unsuspecting lounges of Georgetown and ended up at Mr. Henry's, a gay bar where Tori was invited to play for tips on occasional evenings. In August, she and her father moved in on Mr. Smith's, a lounge run by one Mrs. Reckert who acquiesced to interview and audition Tori for a job. Happy with what she heard, the proprietor hired the young pianist but became somewhat less captivated when she spotted her new entertainer's date of birth on an employment form. Needless to say, trouble with the law was not high on the bar-owner's shopping list, but Dr. Amos was determined; he struck a deal and agreed that he and his wife would be present to chaperon Tori's every performance. This led to Mr. Smith's gaining not one but two new attractions as the handsome reverend standing in the back of the room in his white collar received his fair share of attention. He was not daunted, however, but rather was "delighted" that Tori was not "being hit on."

For Tori, Mr. Smith's was a wonderland. "The daiquiris were going all the time, like ten blenders, coconut, pineapple, peach daiquiris," she says. "They would give me 'virgins' without the booze. You would hear the blenders going all the

At the Wacipi Indian Festival (age 15)

Homecoming Queen December 1980 ('All the nerds voted for me')

Tori was voted 'Choir Flirt' at Montgomery High

time when you'd walk in. I went upstairs to the Tiffany Lounge where I played. I alternated with a guy named Duke Marvin, and he would be playing things like *'I don't want her, you can have her, she's too fat for me'*—sing-a-long songs. *'Sarah, Sarah, sitting in a knitting shop, all day long she sits and knits, all day long she knits and sits'*—and if you sing it real fast and you're drunk you start to say profanities. They all thought that was really funny and I couldn't really understand the punch line, I would always be like, you mean, that's IT? These grown-up people are sitting here getting off on that? It was like, where's Monty Python?" Tori found herself back in the familiar routine of being several girls at once. By day, she was a "friendly nerd" amongst the potentially cruel world of Silver Spring's Eastern Junior High School. She insists to this day that she was invited to parties purely with the understanding that she would provide the musical entertainment. On Friday nights she took on the role of favorite performer in the company of a much older and wiser group. Wearing her sister Marie's polyester pants and more than a touch of make-up, Tori took on the confidence and charisma of a veteran to the stage. The gang at Mr. Smith's welcomed the thirteen-year-old into their world without hesitation, and Tori still cites them today as one of the most supportive and appreciative audiences she has ever had the pleasure to play for. "Being exposed to the gay community at thirteen would change my views forever," Tori says, "and I have stayed close with that community ever since." On Sundays, she moved into yet another realm where her responsibilities (musical and otherwise) demanded a distinctly different Tori. She seemed to change her role models at different hours of the day, from the Magdalene to the Mother Mary, whichever worked best at the moment. Although she was playing everything from Gershwin to Bootsy Collins to Patti Smith at Mr. Smith's, Tori kept up her songwriting. Already attuned to expressing herself through her music, her early songs have a particularly personal slant.

You Too Can Have a Career in Music, a look at ELLEN AMOS

It's a tough business and sometimes I just don't know where to go next. But if I were to quit, I'd never know if I could've made it.

Plugging a record takes time and more time. It's exhausting and not usually rewarding. But when one station decides to play it, all that pushing was worth it.

Many people and teachers don't understand the hours that have to be put in and all the phone calls one has to make just to get on one station. Air time is the only way a record can make it. I'm shooting for local support on the local stations.

Because the record industry is in a slump, they're very selective in whom they sign. Sometimes the only way to catch their ear is to make a name for yourself.

I'm only 17 right now. Time has been pretty good to me. But I would like to have a Top 40 single out before I'm 20. The first single isn't the most important. It's the second single that's so important.

Nothing will stop me. Maybe that sounds like I have a big ego but I don't really. Sure, I know what I can do and I believe in myself. I know how well I could do and I know what I have to work on. If record companies think that you think you're just O.K. they don't want you. You have to be better than just O.K. or they won't sign you on.

I have much to be thankful for—especially my family and that I was lucky enough to be given a musical gift.

Ellen Amos

Princesses

Ellen Amos

Senior **Ellen Amos** continued to further her bright career as a singer when she appeared at the Myrtle Beach Hilton in South Carolina during April.

Most Likley To Succeed

from the Richard Montgomery High School 1981 Yearbook.

Just Ellen

I'm too young for a man

But I'm too old for a boy

So can't we just pretend

That I'm older than I really am

But then, only little girls pretend.

In June of 1978, Dr. Amos moved on to another church, and the family moved into the Rockville United Methodist Church's parsonage. Tori expanded her musical training with voice lessons and thought she'd try acting after developing an obsession for Bette Davis. "It wouldn't have been so bad to die by her hand," she now declares. She performed at the Rockville Summer Theatre as well as in several school productions, most notably as the title role in *Gypsy,* a musical about the life of stripper Gypsy Rose Lee. She also began directing the children's choir at her father's new church, staying up late after her club dates to write musicals for the children. The rather unorthodox sight of Tori in red leather pants coaxing a tune out of fifty youngsters in front of the congregation became a weekly occurrence. Although the kids adored their new musical leader, according to Tori's own mother, "the mothers weren't so thrilled with her." Of course, Mrs. Amos had had years to become accustomed to her daughter's ways; as she says, "even when she was little, she just *loved* to shock us."

News of Tori's talent seemed to be spreading, and she had a full itinerary with gigs at weddings, government functions, and church benefits. In April of 1979 she was invited out to the University of North Dakota Indian Association's Wacipi Festival where she performed along with many others of Native American heritage.

In the fall of 1980, Tori cut her first single with the private pressing of a song cowritten with her brother Mike. The song was entitled "Baltimore," and it was

AT THE DOOR
Formerly The Cellar Door

ellen amos

With
Bill,
Mike,
& Phil

Vocalist

Pianist-Composer

29 December 8 PM
Tuesday — Georgetown
34th & M Sts. N.W.
Washington, D.C. 20007
Reservations — 338-3300

At The Door flyer

The Door gig

THE MYRTLE BEACH HILTON

August 24, 1981

To Whom This May Concern:

This letter is to serve as a full endorsement of Ellen Amos. She comes to you with the highest recommendation the Myrtle Beach Hilton and its guests can offer.

She was originally booked for one month, however, we were so impressed with her extraordinary talent and professionalism that we set a precedent and invited her to return for an additional month. She is very sensitive to her audience - her vocals are beautiful. She has been a tremendous asset to our business.

I wholeheartedly recommend Miss Amos for an entertainment position.

Sincerely,

Conrad Wangeman
Conrad Wangeman
Food & Beverage
CW/eb

Arcadian Shores Myrtle Beach, South Carolina 29577 803/449-7461

Myrtle Beach Hilton recommendation letter

Playing at Washington DC's Sheraton-Carlton Hotel, 1982

written in honor of the city's baseball team, the Baltimore Orioles. A college basketball fanatic who only missed one game on television in three years, she now says "I figured I wasn't whoring too much to do baseball instead of basketball. You know, it's a sister sport; it's got a ball." The single was released on her own label, MEA (her initials). She was then awarded a Citation from the Mayor of Baltimore for "the splendid quality of public service you have rendered."

In an article in the December 1980 edition of the Washington *Post*, seventeen-year-old Tori is quoted as saying, "I want to be a legend." Her father, also interviewed, tells the *Post* that his goal is to "get her into entertainment without her entering into a lifestyle that is self-destructive." Dr. Amos knew that Tori's school friends were spending their free time experimenting with marijuana and getting pregnant, and he intended to keep his daughter so busy that she wouldn't have time to join in.

While most of her fellow high school seniors were accomplishing as little actual work as possible in their final school year, Tori was busier than ever, sandwiching extra music, voice, and drama classes at Montgomery College between her required high school classes. Instructed by her mother not to stop and talk in the halls (an impossibility, apparently), Tori would rush out of one school building and into the family car to be whisked away to another.

After her high school graduation, Tori convinced her parents that a traditional college education would not further her musical career ("Warner Brothers doesn't give a shit about scholastic accomplishment—you know, are you good or do you suck?"), and they agreed that she should take only music-related courses at Montgomery College. Her career, now in its fifth professional year, was moving along at a steady clip. In the summer of 1981 she secured a position at the Hilton hotel in Myrtle Beach, South Carolina, as their chief entertainer. Tori remembers playing six nights a week in the Spring, her term paper due, her parents in the Hilton's office after hours. "I'd come visit them during my break with a virgin

Pina Colada for each one of them. They'd be typing away and arguing with each other over Milton's *Samson Agonistes*. The theological doctor and his wife, the literature major in college, only received a 'C.'" In December she proudly appeared at the Cellar Door, a well-known Washington venue which had presented such talents as John Denver and Neil Young; she was paid by check which, to her amazement, bounced.

Throughout 1982 and 1983 she played everything from the Doors to Barbra Streisand to Beethoven (peppered with a few originals) in the piano lounge and bar of Washington D.C.'s Sheraton-Carlton hotel where "there were a lot of Congressional people so that was a whole different thing. They all had the most beautiful assistants. They would come like 'this is my assistant, meet my assistant,' and I'm like, O.K., hang on a minute, there's gotta be something to this. All these assistants are absolutely drop-dead beautiful with diamonds dripping off their wrists. I don't know. I ain't quite buying it. I ran into the hookers about this time and became friends with particularly one of them who finally had to leave because she felt her life was in danger because she was seeing somebody on the Hill, and she knew too much; and she fled to Japan because of a powerful warlord—she went to go be protected by him, and I never heard from her." (Tori would years later write a song about her entitled "The Wrong Band.") This hospitable establishment was the site of Tori's first exposure to the fickle nature of the entertainment industry when on Independence Day she arrived on the scene in a dress bought especially for the occasion only to find a man in a tuxedo seated on her piano bench. "You've been fired," the hotel manager explained.

Tori, still known as Ellen at this point, had been searching for a name. One night one of her girlfriends, Linda McBride, came to hear her play and brought with her "some guy she was dating; she only saw him for like a week, I can't even remember his name… and so he just looks at me out of the blue, I've never met this guy before and he goes, 'Tori. Your name's Tori,' and I'm like, 'yeah, you're right.' And then we never saw him again. I found out very soon that Tori was a kind of pine tree and so I adopted the name."

While Tori continued writing songs Dr. Amos decided to appeal to an eclectic mix of individuals who had already cracked it in the entertainment industry, and wrote on church stationery to the likes of Michael Jackson, Charlton Heston, and Frank Sinatra (in care of Caesar's Palace, Las Vegas). None save Mr. Heston replied, despite the reverend's dinner invitation to old blue eyes and his wife. Undeterred by the lack of superstar sponsorship, Tori was gaining exposure on her own appearing on local television shows and playing live on local radio stations. Moving on to her own spot as featured performer at Georgetown's Lion's Gate Taverne in the Marbury House hotel, she attracted a slightly hipper audience along with a stack of enthusiastic press clippings. The Washington *Post* prophetically notes that "Amos, who is also occasionally known as Tori, may very well be a famous pop star someday."

Dr. Amos was busy sending demo tapes to every major record label in the United States and abroad, the majority of which resulted in polite form letters with the occasional spark of interest. His indefatigable support paid off when Tori's music caught the ear of producer Narada Michael Walden. In July of 1983 Tori wrote to Mr. Walden in California, saying, "I know you're going on vacation. I always get bored on vacations. So to give you something to do, I'm going to continue to send you a tape every week up until the time I come out there. What can I say—thoughtful is my middle name." Presumably the tapes staved off the vacationing producer's boredom, as in November of 1983 Tori flew to San Francisco to record a demo at Narada's Automatic Studio. With Culture Club and the second British invasion cited as influences, Tori's music had taken a definite turn toward dance and pop, and she was concentrating more on her vocals and on mastering home recording equipment than on the piano.

GEORGETOWN

The
Lions Gate Tavern,
one of the most intimate lounges in Georgetown features the unique talents of entertainer

Ellen Amos

Tues.- Sat. evenings from 7:00 pm-midnight at the Georgetown Marbury House

30th & M St. N.W.
333·3949

MARBURY HOUSE

Marbury House flyer

She returned from the West Coast even more enthusiastic than before, and continued to hone her performance skills nightly at the Marbury House. Overly eager to please, Tori responded to her growing and demanding audience by singing every request that came her way from six P.M. until the wee hours of the morning, and her ardor soon backfired when in July her doctor informed her that she had done serious damage to her vocal cords. He prescribed ten days of total silence, after which he would decide if more drastic measures were needed. Tori's parents decided that the only way to accomplish this would be to whisk their daughter away for ten days to a place where she could not be reached by telephone. As luck would have it, the perfect place presented itself in Dr. Amos's childhood home in the mountains of Southwest Virginia. The next morning Tori and her mother drove to the 100-year-old house and commenced their sojourn of silence. Mrs. Amos recalls, "we had envisioned this ten-day period to be one of great difficulty, but it turned out to be a time of relaxation, healing, and inspiration." Tori communicated with her mother via note-writing, and the two of them spent hours sitting on the old wooden porch listening to the sounds of nature. Upon their return, Tori's doctor declared that she was not in need of surgery but that the singer would have to remember to put herself before her music, which has never happened. "I'm a musician first, a food-lover second, a dirty mouth with feet, and a girl last time I checked."

" HERE. IN MY HEAD "

The passion and the craving that Tori felt in her soul found no home within her strict Christian upbringing. Driven by a profound fear of alienation, Tori forced herself to accept the belief system of her parents and of the church, knowing that to do so was in effect to kill a part of herself. But her passionate self—the part of her that rejected the role model of the Virgin Mary—refused to die, and so what Tori now refers to as "a division of the self" took place. Tori hints at the inner anguish of such a duality of spirit when she states, "If you're divided then you're in continuous torment, because you never allow yourself to fully experience anything."

This wrenching split within her own personality was the only way that Tori could survive. In order to exist in the public world, she created a completely different world inside her head. Her private set of beliefs began to form their own language, bursting forth into the outside world in the form of music. The poet in Tori was born of this passionate being buried within, and the songs which would make Tori famous in the years to come would be her only expression of this inner self. "People don't know where the songs come from when they meet me because I'm so relaxed and centered and balanced and jovial. But I take that stage and that piano and demon girls come out. There are things that I refuse to deal with except through my music; things I will *only* deal with through my music... because I just don't trust humanity that much, and I don't know if I trust me that much. But I trust the songs."

Tori's simultaneous experience of two very different realities, one public and bound by parameters of other people's design and one private and conceived in an altogether different dimension, was a constant in her life. The knowledge that she could give life, through music, to the side of herself that she had suppressed for so many years was hard-won, and the battle was just beginning. Her present-day following recognizes her struggle to bring out this vital part of her psyche. As Tori says, "They know that they are seeing something very personal, and it reminds them of themselves. Many people lock a part of themselves away. It's a bit sacred."

Off to Hollywood

The Kellogg's Just Right *girl*

Y KANT TORI READ

(1 9 8 4 – 1 9 8 9)

On September 10, 1984, Tori left home to move to Los Angeles, diving headlong into what she now refers to as her "rock-chick phase." The move represented freedom "beyond anything I can express. I was a kid in a candy shop. Lemon drops, cinnamon sticks, fire balls, licorice… good thing I know a very good dentist."

Setting up her own little studio in a tiny apartment situated, interestingly enough, behind a church in Hollywood, the twenty-one-year-old set to work immersing herself in the local music scene. With her usual verve and unflagging interest in everyone and everything around her, Tori soon familiarized herself with the best and the worst that L.A. had to offer. Within three weeks, she had assembled a band and had them booked at the downtown Sheraton. Tori's first experience of playing with a group was less than inspiring, as "one showed up drunk. One showed up stoned. One didn't show up at all one night. It was a bummer." Tori decided that, at least to make ends meet, she would have to depend only on herself and began playing solo in a string of Hollywood lounges and bars.

In the true Hollywood tradition, Tori spent a brief and occasionally profitable time in the land of television commercials and residuals. To help pay the rent for her new apartment, Tori found herself in a commercial for Kellogg's Just Right cereal for which she had to cut her hair to a rather less-than-bitchin' length. "But I needed the money," she explains. "They almost gave it to Sarah Jessica Parker. She was down for it and I was down for it, and the director chose me because I could really play the piano. She looked like she was faking it—well, she was faking it. But she's a good actress, so you know, she almost faked it better than I did it for real."

The Y Kant Tori Read *band: Brad Cobb, Matt Sorum, Tori, and Steve Caton*

Recording Y Kant Tori Read *with producer Joe Chicarelli*

After spending Christmas with her family back in Maryland, Tori returned to Los Angeles only to meet with tragedy in the form of a member of her audience to whom she agreed to give a lift home one night. The horror Tori experienced as she was held hostage and raped was too profound to express, and after calling her mother who immediately flew to Los Angeles to be with her daughter, Tori vowed never to speak of it again. Closing a door in her mind as tightly as she could, she moved resolutely forward.

The next few years were spent working, working, working, and on occasion the term "starving artist" took on an all-too-vivid meaning as Tori drained her substantial savings on recording equipment and studio time. Playing with seemingly countless musicians over the course of these years did not dissipate Tori's determination to put together a band that would catapult her to stardom. In a 1985 letter home to her parents she reveals, "I have to accept that the girl and her piano are dead. That time in history is over."

Finally, in 1987, Tori's career took the turn she had been working toward. Atlantic Records decided to pay attention to the determined singer/songwriter and her revolving band. Tori Amos signed the long-awaited record deal she had been dreaming about since she'd picked up her older brother's *Sgt. Pepper's* album at the age of four. Recording the album under the supervision of Joe Chicarelli, a producer with an unusual list of artists on his resume including Frank Zappa, Pat Benatar, and Oingo Boingo, was literally a dream come true. She remembers now that a friend, Steve Himelfarb, an assistant engineer who would sneak her into studios to play the pianos, warned her that "'getting the record deal is only the first step, it's like you've just climbed the wall, and then there's France, and you have to cross the whole country...' He certainly was right. But I wasn't listening to him, I wasn't having it."

"The *Y Kant Tori Read* band had fallen apart being pulled by too many outside opinions, and I was too obsessed about making it to take a stand." Steve Farris

Taking a break at the Amos family farm in Virginia

(previously of Mr. Mister), Kim Bullard (who had played with Poco), and Matt Sorum who would later play drums for Guns N' Roses, all played on the album. Singles for "The Big Picture" and "Cool on Your Island" were released, along with a video for "The Big Picture." The video—directed by Marty Collner, famous now for all of the Aerosmith videos and the early Whitesnake videos—opens with a now almost unrecognizable Tori confronting a Los Angeles police officer who is giving her a parking ticket. "Wait a minute— somebody broke into my car, took my underwear—that's gross!" Tori protests. The officer replies, "I'm sorry ma'am, I'm writing you a ticket; you're illegally parked," before walking away only to display a red garter belt in the back pocket of his uniform. The video moves on to Tori at the peak of her rock-chick era dancing and singing her way through a set of the streets of East L.A., stopping only to spray-paint graffiti on a few cars and one young man. As Charles Aaron puts it in the October 1994 issue of *SPIN* magazine, "*Y Kant Tori Read* was *Streets of Fire* without the the nifty soundstage and silly villians, and after [the album] stiffed, she tottered away in her plastic thigh-high boots."

Y Kant Tori Read was released at the end of May 1988. Reviews of the record were hard to come by; in fact, most of the journals that reviewed it were hard to come by. The *Potomac Gazette* featured a photo of the album cover (Tori sporting a push-up bra and a very big sword) encaptioned, "She is the daughter of a local minister." In this article Tori refers to herself as "Peter Pan in leather." A review printed a bit further from home in the British heavy-metal magazine *Kerrang!* presumes that Tori's *nom de plume* is in fact Tori Read; the reviewer Derek Oliver goes on to praise the album closing with the prophesy that "for most folk,

Y
KANT
TORI
READ

COOL
ON
YOUR
ISLAND

Y KANT TORI READ

however, Tori's music is just too damn bizarre and she is destined, I fear, to enter the realms of eternal obscurity. Pity."

"That was where all the illusions came crumbling down," Tori remembers. "It had all become about being accepted instead of making music I believed in. I bought into the whole trip. There's no question about it; I bought the whole thing. It all became about making it, like that was going to give me some sense of self, that was going to fill this empty hole inside. So, when it started to fail, that's when I understood that the whole industry was based on sand; it's not based on rock. If you buy into the fame trip, then you've really lost sight of why you're making music. Fame has just got to be a sideline. It goes with the territory and once you understand that it's a bit like mosquitos. If you're going to go live in the wilderness there's going to be mosquitos."

Had the record-buying public had any idea of the years of effort put into getting this album cut, perhaps they would have given it a spin. Regardless, Tori's debut barely saw the light of day and was relegated by *Billboard* to the realm of "bimbo music." Within three weeks of its release it was dead in the water, and Tori was crippled with confusion. Tori would later say that she became "like jelly on the kitchen floor" and would spend hours staring at the flecks in the linoleum, getting up only to make the journey to the bathroom.

The pivotal point came one day when Tori walked into Hugo's Restaurant in full *Y Kant Tori Read* regalia. "The record was failing, *Billboard* had called me a bimbo and it was really going down the toilet… it was an industry failure, and everybody was very aware of it. There were two different record company acquaintances there—they weren't from my label—and I remember going up to them and they were snickering. One of them was snickering, and one of them was ignoring me. And it hit me at that moment that I was a joke, that I had become a joke. And in that second I went back to being four years old. I could just feel my four-year-old in my body going, 'This is not what I envisioned.' To

Tori, Cindy Marble (with son Isaac), and Eric Rosse

go from a prodigy to a joke at twenty-four was very hard to accept. But I walked out of that restaurant with water-proof mascara, not a lot of dignity, went home and took off my make-up, threw on a T-shirt, and pulled off my thigh-high boots."

She then went straight to her friend Cindy Marble's place. Cindy owned an old piano, and Tori sat down and began to play while her friend sat in the corner of the room. Tori's hands did not leave the keys for five hours until her friend said, "You have to do this, this is what you were meant to do." Tori remembers, "I said, 'Cindy, I can't. Because if they cut this up, there would be nothing left of me.' And she said, 'Well, what's left of you now? At least have your dignity, at least you can walk away going, "This is what I do, and I do it well, and I know I do it well and that's enough." Now you're not even showing anybody what you really do.'" The next morning Tori woke up and rented a piano which she had delivered to her apartment that same day.

LITTLE EARTHQUAKES

(1989–1992)

In the fall of 1989, Atlantic decided, according to Tori "to roll the dice one more time with me" and gave her until March of 1990 to put together a new albumful of songs. Tori was shedding her tough rock-chick ego, and a more internal, if slightly more fragile, facet of her personality seemed to be cautiously emerging. Appealing to nature to aid the healing process, she spent time near Carmel in California and with her family at the farm in Virginia.

Tori started all over again in the little Hollywood "hut" she called home. Having jump-started her confidence, she felt she was on track again when a visit from Doug Morris, President of Atlantic, put an end to that. After listening to a few of the new songs, Tori remembers, "He said, 'What is this shit?'" and left with the less-than-encouraging comment of, " 'I just don't know what I'm going to do with you. I thought you were going to give me "Rocket Man." I mean, you said you were writing songs around a piano, so where's "Rocket Man" ?' " This brief visitation pushed the frail songwriter back into the canyon of despair as surely as if someone had pried her hands from the edge of a cliff, and she spent another three months without touching a piano. Turning to guitarist Steve Farris and penning a tune called "The Underwear Is Black," Tori started to pull out her hairspray bottle again, until Cindy Marble and Nancy Shanks, ever-faithful friends, screamed, "Tori, oh my god, you can't do this. Steve is great, but Lita Ford does Lita Ford a little better than you do."

After yet another dark period of painful self-examination, Tori decided to appeal to the muses that had provided her with so much inspiration and companionship back in the days before she knew what a record deal was. She proceeded to create a "faerie ring—like the old Celtic ring" on her living room floor. "I brought in sticks and things from the outside, from nature, and put the things that I was

Starting over again (note the Y Kant Tori Read *sword on the wall)*

most connected with inside the ring. Whenever anyone came in, they had to step over my magic ring . . . my friends came by and looked. They didn't say much to me. They all knew I was doing my faerie shit." Adding a set of empty envelopes to the ring, Tori sat inside the ring and began to write again, vowing to give each envelope a song title. "One of the first envelopes to get a name was 'Take to the Sky'" (*This house is like Russia / with eyes old and grey / you got me moving in a circle / I dyed my hair red today*). During this period Tori called the record company to let them know that she would be submitting a brand new set of songs before the end of March, insisting that this time, "I'm going to turn in what I feel is me—Tori—my music, my lyrics." She then undertook the soul-searching and often heart-rending task so beautifully documented in "Silent All These Years," and turned in the same songs she played for Doug Morris that day months before, thinking "he won't remember."

And so began a tug-of-war with the five-foot-two-inch redhead holding on for dear life at one end of a rope securely anchored on the other by a multimillion-dollar corporate team so sure of their success they played in three-piece suits. Early in 1990, apparently worried about the likelihood of their receiving a set of hits by the March deadline, Atlantic contacted Tori to inform her that they were sending someone to see her to give her a bit of a boost with the lyrics and music. "That just usurped my confidence even more. I said, 'They don't think I'm capable.'" Hence Davitt Sigerson, future producer of half of the tracks on the *Little Earthquakes* album, arrived quite literally on Tori's doorstep. He didn't stay for long, however. After listening to her play "Take to the Sky," "Leather," and a few other pieces, he proclaimed that Tori did not need any help and gave both artist and record company the conviction to move ahead with the album. After several weeks in the studio recording the eleven songs born of Tori's faerie ring, the tape was sent up to the bigwigs at Atlantic.

Tori plays at her father's church, Christmas Eve 1990

In the London flat

"I waited, and waited, and waited, and finally they rejected the master tape, with a comment that there wasn't a hit among them… they waited until two or three days before Christmas to tell me the album was unacceptable." Rather than being crushed, Tori was infuriated. The knowledge she had gained by digging deeper when at her lowest point and the voice she had thus excavated had given her strength, and she held on tight and persevered. "I started again," she explains. She and Eric Rosse recorded four more tracks in his home studio, "because we had blown the budget. They were reluctant to give us any more money." These four tracks were "Girl," "Precious Things," "Tear in Your Hand," and "Little Earthquakes." Rosse remembers, "We did those on the shortest shoestring of a budget that you could imagine. You couldn't even tie two shoes together with the length of shoestring that we did that on. It showed me how much can be done for very little if you have a tremendous amount of energy and a tremendous amount of commitment to see it through." Another visit from Doug Morris interrupted the recording, but after hearing "Girl," he encouraged them to carry on with his blessing.

It was now early 1991, and the album-in-progress comprised ten songs. The struggle with the record company came to an end as the corporate team let go of their end of the rope and sent Tori flying over the Atlantic Ocean, still tugging. Not sure what they had on their hands, they had decided, with the approval of Tori's manager Arthur Spivak, to ship this particular package to their British counterparts at East West Records in London. Tori was thrilled. "I took to London like a duck taking to water," she recalls. A candlelit private audition for Max Hole, President of East West, convinced both the songwriter and the captivated executive that she was where she belonged. Tori was set up in a flat belonging to someone else and filled with the truant owner's possessions, but she had a piano and was only a few blocks away from her new record company's offices.

"It was a great adventure," she says now, "because I had no fears about England,

I didn't know the word No, I wasn't intimidated. I would have been a history teacher if I wouldn't have been a suet specialist, if I didn't know the piano. The Norman invasion is kind of my specialty, so I kind of went as an historian, if you can believe that. England was about going to Canterbury, walking through the streets of London, drinking in the history, drinking in the past, taking the trains everywhere I could, trying to read and remember what happened from the earth. Drinking in information, tapping into the land, trying to smell it. Walking on the moors going up to York, the Brontë land. Trying to just immerse myself in the literature, trying to remember, because I spent a lot of lifetimes there, and I knew that. I was just trying to recapture parts of myself, my power, my memories. And I did it through my knowledge of history. I would try and recapture certain periods of time. The big period of time for me in England was the eleventh century, the twelfth, thirteenth, and fourteenth centuries. Those were the times that really got me. I still argue to this day that Richard III did not kill the princes, and I'm so passionate about that; I just get so passionate about how he was misunderstood. It's funny how you don't lose certain perspectives on things. And I know which side I stood on back then."

A plan of action was devised; Tori would test the waters by playing at a few small clubs in London ("I felt I was going back in time," she now remembers) and this would create a bit of interest. The concocters of this strategy were pleased to discover that their guinea pig was no novice when it came to self-promotion and stage presence. Tori's versatile voice and expert hand at the keys startled more than a few punters who considered the pub's piano a convenient place to rest their pints of lager or something to lean against while carrying on a conversation. After opening for better-known groups in small venues like the Mean Fiddler, the Borderline, the Dominion, the Jazz Cafe, and the Troubadour—where Al Stewart (*Year of the Cat*) had taken Tori when he was touring the U.K.—word got out, and quick. Tori showed the Brits a bit of

Southern hospitality and gave private performances to key critics in her flat. Lee Ellen Newman, head of press at East West records became Tori's confidante and probably the closest person to her, having been there from the beginning. Curious music-lovers and even more curious journalists clutching their pads and pens began following Tori on her tour of London's many cheap and cheerful acoustic venues. No one was disappointed, and everyone got more than they bargained for, especially the press who soon discovered that the girl at the piano's alarming openness didn't stop with her songwriting.

That summer, Tori went alone to see a new film entitled *Thelma and Louise* at a London cinema. During the scene where Geena Davis's character is being raped, the horrifying experience Tori had gone through six years before in Los Angeles burst from her subconscious to the forefront of her mind. Seated outside the Mean Fiddler in North London later that afternoon just a few hours before her gig, she wrote "Me and a Gun" (*It was me and a gun and a man on my back and I sang "holy holy" as he buttoned down his pants*) and sang the cathartic song *a capella* for the first time that same night.

During this period, Tori met up with two very interesting people who both became important friends to her and with whom she would collaborate; both would interpret her music and her philosophy through their own art.

Elyse Taylor at East West orchestrated the bringing together of Tori and a photographer by the name of Cindy Palmano. After listening to Tori's music and to Tori, Cindy created the artwork for the *Little Earthquakes* album. The little blue piano inside the wooden box with Tori "came from my boyfriend's childhood," explains Palmano. *Alice in Wonderland* was the inspiration for the unusual dimensions. Cindy's beautiful work would visualize Tori's music in many ways in the coming months and years. The photographer explains that she is not inspired by particular lyrics or by precise descriptions from Tori, but says, "it's much less specific than that," and that Tori "talks to me at random, and then I present her with a set of ideas as a result of it—we have a chat."

Tori with mom and dad down the local pub

In the English countryside

Tori's friendship with Neil Gaiman, the author of *Sandman*, D.C. Comics' fantastically popular and unusual series, began in a slightly less direct fashion. After including a reference to Neil and to the Dream King, the main character in the *Sandman* series, in "Tear in Your Hand," Tori had a friend deliver a tape of the song to Neil at a San Diego comic convention. Neil, who receives many tapes from fans which he says usually "magically become blank tapes" remembers, "I listened to the first three or four tracks, and I was in love. It wasn't *Little Earthquakes*, it was sort of half *Little Earthquakes* and half what wound up being B-sides—things like 'Flying Dutchman' and 'Take to the Sky' and 'Sweet Dreams' and 'Upside Down.' But it was very obvious that musically I was a fan by the time I'd finished listening to the first few tracks. In fact it was ages before I spotted the '*me and Neil'll be hangin' out with the DREAM KING Neil says hi by the way*'—that came much later." After listening to the tape, Neil, who lived in London, called Tori up, and the first of many wonderful conversations commenced. Tori now insists that the two knew each other in a past life. Neil states, "we were old friends immediately. Whether you want to view that as fact or metaphor, that is very much true."

One of the few eyewitnesses to Tori's early gigs in London, Neil remembers the first time he met her in person when he was one of an audience of four people at the Canal Brasserie in London's Notting Hill. The other three members of the crowd were, according to Neil, "a roadie person," a reporter from *Melody Maker,* and Lee Ellen Newman. The owner of the brasserie was also present, but as he was having his birthday dinner with a few friends around a table he isn't counted. Neil recalls, "Tori waved at me when I came in—recognizing me, and went straight off into 'Tear in Your Hand.' It was really lovely. She performed 'Me and a Gun'—it was stunning." A review of the Canal Brasserie performance appeared in the October 12, 1991, issue of *Melody Maker,* and reviewer David Stubbs proclaimed that, "Live, Tori's music makes for absolutely compelling,

but uncomfortable listening… I feel like I've cheated on my wife, although I haven't. Honestly." Gaiman has since used Tori's song lyrics and quotes from their discussions in the *Sandman* series, and one of the main characters, Delirium, has taken on more than a few mental and physical attributes of Tori's. Neil says, "Delirium was created before I met Tori, but they steal shamelessly from each other."

Having proven that the British public was most definitely interested in their new acquisition, East West set to work laying the groundwork for the album's release early the next year. Doug Morris flew over to meet with Max Hole to hear the final of *Little Earthquakes*; Tori, requested by the two in a London restaurant to play something for them, poured out "China." The two men were captivated and decreed that the song must be part of the album. Tori worked feverishly with Ian Stanley to record "China" and to put the finishing touches on the forthcoming album.

"Me and a Gun" was also recorded with Ian Stanley and released on an EP featuring the single "Silent All These Years" in November 1991. The heart-wrenching songs cut through the dance oriented "Madchester" British music scene like a butcher knife and seemingly struck a more personal chord with a public saturated with the detached beat of techno. England's discerning music fans pricked up their ears and brushed aside a few of the latest bright young things to make space for the slightly disturbing but ultimately much more interesting American and her piano. In late November, Tori performed "Silent All These Years" with a band on the *Jonathan Ross Show*, the U.K.'s closest equivalent to America's *Late Night with David Letterman;* it was her first British television appearance. Tori recalls, "I almost ruined the whole thing. I was looking at that girl on the T.V. screen and thinking, if I stop, will she keep playing? If she stops, do I keep playing? It was all live, and for three seconds I froze in the middle of *Silent,* and I thought I was never going to get it together again. I just panicked."

The Little Earthquakes *piano*

Yet another of Tori's alter-egos, Delirium, hanging out with the Dream King in Sandman
(Used by permission, Copyright 1992-93 DC Comics)

September '91, London

In a land bereft of an overabundance of radio stations and not yet saturated by MTV, the music press takes on a huge importance and is often the first and only exposure the record-buying public has to an artist before trundling off to a local record store. The U.K. music papers delighted in the talkative, open-to-a-fault, and downright strange songstress. Building up to and immediately after the January 13, 1992, U.K. release of the aptly titled *Little Earthquakes*, which debuted at number 15 in the charts, a rash of enthusiastic articles popped up in every newspaper and magazine even remotely devoted to music. Comparisons with the likes of Kate Bush, Janis Ian, Joni Mitchell, Sinead O'Conner, Margaret Mary O'Hara, and Patti Smith flew like french fries at a food fight, usually followed by an apology. Quickly giving up the attempt to categorize the "new" talent, the journalists gave in to temptation and celebrated the many ways that she *wasn't* like anyone else. In fact, they started broadcasting her insanity. The *New Musical Express* declared her a "Grade A, Class One, Turbo-driven Fruitcake" in its January 11 edition. The February 1992 cover of *Q* shows a photo of a pensive-looking Tori with the emboldened caption "WEIRD CHICK—On the couch with Tori Amos."

Not only did the solo artist have a personality big enough for a ten-piece band, she made wonderful music. Using words like "brilliant," "sensual," and "inspired," the music press stirred up a burgeoning interest. In the January 4, 1992, edition of *Melody Maker*, reviewer Jon Wilde writes, "It would seem that Tori Amos has nothing to declare but her own, um, (c'mon man, cough it up)… genius."

Tori and Cindy meantime, been very closely to stirring video for Years." This was  Palmano had, in the working together create the beautifully "Silent All These Cindy Palmano's first venture into moving pictures, having been primarily a still photographer before

from the Little Earthquakes *album cover shoot*

this project, and her approach resulted in a breathtaking vision of the emotions inherent in the song. Citing her as one of the most important influences in her life, Tori says "Cindy helped to put my vision out to the world, and without her it would never have been interpreted the way that it was. She has such a pure eye that she was able to go in there and capture my soul on film."

The album was released by Atlantic in the United States in February and received the all-important MTV boost in March when the network broadcasted a "New Artist Spotlight" and tagged the "Silent" video a "Buzz Clip." The April issue of *Rolling Stone* called her songs "smart, melodic and dramatic" and the album "a gripping debut" as well as throwing yet another comparison into the pot with Siouxsie Sioux of Siouxsie and the Banshees. *Billboard* highlighted the album as a "Power Pick" at its position of 110 in its second week in the charts, and featured an interview with producer Davitt Sigerson who had recently been appointed President of Polydor.

Tori's music had the capacity to get under the skin of even seasoned, jaded music industry insiders, and once she roped them in, they were in for the duration. John Witherspoon, Tori's tour manager, recalls the first time he saw Tori play in London in 1992, noting, "I go to a lot of shows obviously 'cause I do it for a living, but if I go to them when I'm not working I *never* stay… I'll always, you know, kind of see half of it and then disappear. This was the first show I'd ever been to where I actually sat and watched the whole show right through to the end; I was really fascinated." So fascinated, in fact, that he went backstage afterwards afterwards and discovered that Tori's then tour manager Graham Cooper was moving on to work with They Might Be Giants. Several phone calls to Arthur later, John finally met up with Tori a week or so afterward in Frankfurt, and a great friendship began.

Press and professional interest aside, Tori's music was becoming a constant companion to an ever-growing group of fans who identified with the songwriter

on a very personal level. Each of the twelve songs contained on *Little Earthquakes* tells an intimate story, and each seems to musically manifest one of the girls Tori found within her own chameleon-like personality. The opening track, "Crucify" (*got enough guilt to start my own religion*), seeks to exorcise the coward in the girl who crucifies herself daily in the struggle to please rather than standing up for herself. When the song first came to be written, Tori said, "a door opened and the demons started to show up." "Girl" laments sweetly on her tendency to be whatever was expected of her (*everybody else's girl/maybe one day she'll be her own*). The aching refrain of the title track (*Give me life, give me pain, give me myself again*) cries out for the real, inner girl. The album flies over a rough terrain, swooping down to explore valleys and climbing up to exalt in mountaintops, and stops along the way to alight on the subjects of death, religion, sex, childhood, and betrayal. In the first record company bio East West sent out, Tori reveals that the songs on her upcoming album represent "all my fifty different personalities called back home and melted into one."

It was now time for Tori to draw on yet another of her personas and wow the world on stage. Officially kicking off at London's Shaw Theatre on January 29, a year-long world tour that would have Tori traverse the globe until the very end of 1992 began. Hopping from city to city in England and Scotland throughout February to play to well-primed audiences gave Tori and her entourage just a hint of the pandemonium that was to follow. After all, if the reserved British fans were unwilling to let Tori off the stage, what would the screaming masses in good old America have in store?

Four gigs in Germany followed in early March, and as Tori's sound manager Ian Thorpe said, the fans seemed to believe they possessed "the God-given right to expect her to play forever." The tour pace was speedy, to say the least, and in the middle of the month Tori jumped over to Amsterdam for a one night spot. The next night she played to an enthusiastic crowd in Rome, and her music was

Live at the Birchmere Club in Alexandria, Virginia, April 22, 1992

televised along with an interview subtitled in Italian. One can only wonder what the translator made of Tori's usual madcap diatribe.

Tori returned to England in April to perform a few select shows before saying good-bye to London for the rest of the year. Her first U.S. appearance was on April 20 at New York City's famous folk venue the Bottom Line, where the usually noisy crowd fell into a bemused trance and the Manhattan waitresses (not renowned for their sensitivity) seemed to tip-toe through the tiny tables. A few tracks filmed live at this performance would later make their way into the *Little Earthquakes* long-form video. Two days later Tori made her first U.S. network television appearance by belting out "Crucify" to a suitably subdued David Letterman.

Eighteen nights of performing live in the United States followed with Tori popping up to Canada twice before ending up in familiar territory in Los Angeles. What next? Australia, of course, to play down under in Melbourne and Sydney to captivated Aussie audiences not used to such prompt visits from hot new American artists. The gregarious singer appeared on Australian television eight times in as many days, talking and performing on *The Midday Show, The Afternoon Show, Tonight Live,* and *The World Tonight* (apparently Australian viewers are not early risers) among others.

Tori had agreed to undertake a non-stop four-month tour of the United States commencing at the end of July, on the condition that she receive a little "treat" in the form of a trip to Asia, Isreal, and Iceland. She spent a day each in Seoul and Taipei at the tailend of May, sandwiched in four more German dates, and spent the last days of June in Tel Aviv. The month of June also saw Tori's television appearance on Britain's *Top of the Pops,* traditionally the stepping stone to fame for artists ranging from the Beatles and the Stones to the Smiths.

While her fans in the Northern hemisphere were sunning themselves at the beach, Tori was strutting across glaciers in Iceland and hanging out with Björk, the

On a glacier in Iceland

At the MTV Awards with mom and dad

Tori and John Witherspoon

former lead singer for the Sugarcubes, in Reykjavík. The frozen land left an indelible impression on her because "that's where they still speak the original Norse language; it's the only territory that still speaks it. I have a very strong connection with the Vikings."

Tori was then plopped smack in the middle of America on July 30 in Louisville, Kentucky, to begin a truly grueling four months of straight touring throughout the country. Bringing with her two trusted mates, her tour manager John Witherspoon and sound manager Ian Thorpe, Tori hit the road. For most audiences, this would be the most intimate live musical contact they had ever experienced. Braving the hushed and expectant crowds with only a piano for company on otherwise empty stages, Tori presented a stripped-down, no frills show, and the ticket-holders sat stock-still, almost afraid to breathe lest they break the spell. Writhing on her piano stool, in a world of her own one moment and sending a piercing and all-knowing look into the heart of the audience the next, Tori threw the concept of a conventional rock concert right out the front door and kicked it down the street.

Showing off her skills as a born performer, she flitted from heart-searching intensity to light-hearted banter, and the crowd was besotted. According to John Witherspoon, Tori may be a born performer, but she has a "terrible sense of direction." He recalls the end of one performance when Tori walked off the wrong side of the stage "and all it was on the other side of the stage was a brick wall, but a brick wall with a curtain in front of it, and she actually stood behind the curtain . . . she thought she couldn't be seen but underneath the curtain you could see her shoes."

After a month and a half of performing almost every night, Tori took a few days off and then headed to Los Angeles for the MTV Awards on September 9 with a proud mother and father at her side. Tori had been nominated for Breakthrough Video, Best Cinematography, and Best Female Video with Cindy Palmano's "Silent All These Years" video, as well as for the Best New Artist award.

The Amoses didn't blink an eye at the wacky world of rock and roll assembled at the awards ceremony. Tori introduced her mother to Anthony Keidis of the Red Hot Chili Peppers in the midst of his showing her his tatoos, and the ensuing conversation between Mrs. Amos and the band's bass player Flea can only be guessed at. Tori and her parents shared a taste in hotels with Pearl Jam, and Dr. Amos informed his daughter that he'd "had a chat with 'Pearl'" in the hotel lobby and found them to be "a real nice group of guys."

The very next night Tori appeared on the *Arsenio Hall Show* to perform "Silent All These Years." She spent the remainder of September supporting her "children" (her terminology for her songs) in Utah; California; New Orleans; Alabama; back at her stomping ground in Washington, D.C.; Virginia; North Carolina; West Virginia; Tennessee; Georgia; Texas; New Mexico; Colorado; and Arizona. Alternately flying or driving, if time allowed, Tori and John would spend traveling time listening to the multitude of tapes aspiring songwriter-fans had beseechingly handed to Tori during her backstage soirées.

Although on the earlier British leg of the tour Tori was able to bring a piano along with her, in America she had to pick pianos up along the way, making do with what was available. For someone who holds the belief that every piano has its own personality, this was an opportunity to make a lot of new acquaintances, but it certainly wasn't easy to sit down to a new piano just a few hours before sharing the stage with it.

The September 12 show at the Lumberyard Cafe in Mobile, Alabama, proved to be quite an adventure. Apparently, although Tori's voice had to compete with the sounds of glasses breaking and barroom skirmishes, it was the quietest the venue had ever been. John Witherspoon began to lose patience and told a particularly loud member of the audience to quiet down in no uncertain terms. He had, unfortunately, chosen the chief of police who proceeded to show him his gunshot wounds and demanded some respect while threatening to shut the

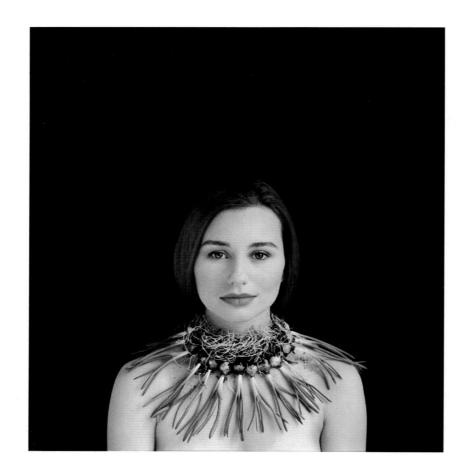

show down. John finds this bizarre episode very funny "in retrospect," but asserts, "at the time it wasn't! Actually I couldn't believe it. It was so unreal, it was like being in some kind of film. I was expecting Robert De Niro from *Cape Fear* to come around the corner at some point." These occasional glitches aside, Tori's summer tour snowballed its way into the fall and early winter. Playing exclusively in small venues meant sold-out shows, but Tori was determined that the intimacy of her performances should not get lost in larger halls. An early morning flight, a live radio performance, and two or three interviews were a regular day's work— all before the 4:00 soundcheck, the two hours alone on stage, and the post-show mayhem.

Tori found herself elected "the President of Victims Anonymous" without even having to run for office, and was often expected to offer instant therapy to dozens of fans who had been saving up their problems for her ears only. Others seemed content to wait for hours for the chance to offer a heartfelt "thank you" without even pausing for an autograph. Tori's willingness to talk with all and sundry at midnight, every night, caused her manager Arthur Spivak more than a little concern, but Tori refused to leave until every autograph had been signed and every fan had been hugged.

Fans of Tori Amos seem to be as diverse a group as a musician could hope to attract. They range in age from six-year-old piano students to their sixty-year-old teachers who both count "China" as one of their favorite pieces. They seemingly represent every nationality and every personality on the planet. And they all seem to want to meet each other, judging by the number of fanzines and fan clubs if not by the impromptu conventions that take place backstage, inside, and outside every Tori concert. With two official fanzines, America's *Really Deep Thoughts* and the U.K.'s *Take to the Sky*, one official fan club, *Upside Down*, and even an Internet computer mailing list also entitled *Really Deep Thoughts* founded in early 1992, up-to-the-minute information and opinions about Tori (and anything even vaguely connected to her) is easily accessible.

from the China *video*

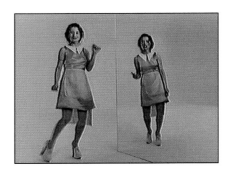

from the Crucify *video*

from the Winter *video*

from the Winter *video*

The *Little Earthquakes* long-form video was released in October 1992. This collection features Cindy Palmano's beautiful videos for "Crucify," "China," "Winter," and of course "Silent All These Years," along with live performances shot at New York City's Bottom Line, at a concert in Rotterdam, Holland, and "Me and a Gun" as sung for MTV Asia. This video is quite a treasure as it captures the unique atmosphere of Tori playing live and brings together four examples of Cindy Palmano's vision of Tori's music. The video for "China," shot at a rocky beach in North Cornwall, England, has as a central image Tori seated on a rock amongst the crashing waves playing a piano built entirely of stones. "Winter," a song that reflects on Tori's childhood relationship with her father (*when you gonna love you as much as I do*), is treated in a nostalgic light. The video is simple and stark, alternating between Tori dancing with a group of children and Tori dressed in white, in a white room, playing a white piano. The entire compilation is tied together by Tori's commentary on, among other things, her songs, monsters, enchiladas, and adolescence, recorded backstage in a very informal setting.

In November of 1992 the *Little Earthquakes* tour came to a close back in the Southern half of the globe. Australians flocked to the Perth, Melbourne, and Sydney shows, and Tori rounded her travels off with a final performance in Auckland, New Zealand. She then ensured that the world wouldn't forget about her by completing a quick "personal appearance" tour granting interviews in the U.K., France, and the States. Tori attended the U.K.'s *Q* Magazine Awards in November, at which she was presented with the "Best New Act" award. The ceremonies also presented her with the long-awaited opportunity to disclose to Robert Plant, in person, her adolescent dreams of losing her virginity to him. He reportedly replied, "Don't let a few years come through your wishes and my ability." This stint also included a performance of "Crucify" and an interview with Jay Leno on the January 12, 1993, *Tonight Show* back in the United States.

During this time Tori visited Vienna, where her favorite piano, the Bösendorfer, has been built by hand since 1835. Having secured an endorsement from Bösendorfer, the company would be providing Tori with their pianos for use on tour and in the studio. The craftsmen there described the making of these beautiful instruments, beginning with the choosing of the wood from forests which Bösendorfer carefully replants every year, and showed Tori into the sanding room whose walls are covered with pictures of naked women to inspire the workman in their creation of the body of the piano.

UNDER THE PINK

(1993–1994)

Meanwhile, Tori's faerie muses had been eagerly awaiting a chance to come out and play. A new set of songs were "insisting" that Tori pay them some attention. "They kind of stalk me, and when I just throw a line on them to try and get them out of my life they become pretty vicious. Because they won't accept me lessening them, just because I'm uncomfortable. The songs just hang out, you know, they come in and move in. To me the songs already exist, I'm just an interpreter for them. Yes, because of my experiences they're going to come through my filter, and that's going to change how I see them. But they already exist in a certain form, and I'm just trying to take them to the third dimension—maybe the fourth really, because I'd like to think my work taps into the fourth dimension, not just three dimensions."

Apparently being a conduit for her music has its drawbacks. "I can't just force them to come, I can't just write something at gunpoint, I don't know how to do that. If the songs don't grace me with their presence, then I'm fucked. There's just no forcing them."

Tori's music is an expression of who she is and who she has been. She says, "My work is inspired by different people. As far as my intimate relationships with men they're very, very personal to me, and I consider them sacred. I won't reveal those things. Their secrets are safe with me as I hope mine are with them."

In order to remove herself from all outside influences Tori decided to build a studio in the middle of nowhere. Nowhere turned out to be Taos, New Mexico, and the atmosphere inherent in the gorgeous desert landscape and in the 150-year-old hacienda where the album that was to become *Under the Pink* was recorded brought its own influences to the next set of songs. Dubbed the "fish house" because of the pervading odor borrowed from crates of seafood the

The "Bells for Her" piano muffled by blankets

Laundry!

Eric Rosse

recording equipment had been packed next to during shipment, the hacienda refused to stay out of the recording process. Tori has since expanded on the theory that the tape picked up more than just her voice and the piano, but also recorded the layers of history that had passed through the house, saying, "When I went to New Mexico I felt the past from the Pueblo nation. You stand out on those plains, and you just see them coming over the hill, you see the horses coming over the hill, and that land is still alive with those memories, the Southwest, that's one reason that I was drawn to go record there."

Eric Rosse coproduced all of the tracks on *Under the Pink* and enlisted the help of two engineers, Bev Jones for the piano/vocals and Paul McKenna for the bass and drums. He also discovered the hacienda. "I had this bizarre calling to go to Taos; I guess it was about a year before we made the record, and I went there for three days, and the next time I went there I went there location scouting for the studio. So, it was a strange thing—I really can't explain it, honestly. It just wanted to sort of happen. And the hacienda happened by accident. It was within the last hour of a two week location search where I'd come up absolutely empty-handed, and just by chance someone knew a friend who was a friend of a friend of a friend and this place was becoming available, so…" So, setting up a studio in the middle of the desert sounds like a wonderful idea, but realistically it presented a bit of a problem. Likening the process to organizing a film shoot on location, Eric was in charge of arranging for equipment to be shipped and musicians to be flown (and driven the 150 or so miles from the nearest airport) to the house in Taos. "It was horrendous. It was a nightmare," he recalls. "It was my nightmare, yes, absolutely. And just occasionally it became everyone else's nightmare when technical things would go wrong and there was no one really around to fix them. But, as horrendous as it was on the technical side and as far as the logistics were concerned, it was overbalanced on a creative side, so the atmosphere more than made up for any nightmares that occurred."

Tori and Eric listen to the latest recording

Tori listens, for the first time, to the string section recorded for "Yes, Anastasia"

Unusual surroundings often inspire unusual approaches, and Tori and Eric dabbled in quite a bit of experimentation when creating the new album's songs. Most dramatically was Eric and Phil Shenale's complete dismantling and reassembly of the old upright piano responsible for the ancient-sounding tones in "Bells For Her." Eric says, gleefully, "We detuned it and smashed the soundboard with hammers and muted strings and changed tunings." Tori also became very interested in working with paradoxes, mixing the acoustic piano with industrial loops.

Tori credits Eric's "madness" for the profusion of unusual sounds and effects on the album, recalling that at one point there were tin cans of food sitting on the strings and styrofoam stuffed under the keys. "We kind of deconstructed pianos," Eric explains. "I wanted to create an atmosphere with the internal workings of pianos and record them in an interesting sort of way, because for me it was a representation of what goes on inside of her. We rolled steel balls on the strings of the Bösendorfer—large ball bearings—and bounced them on the strings and yelled into the soundboard and did all kinds of things. Some of it didn't make it on to the record but it was all part of a process which lead us to creating some of the subtler textures on the record."

The freedom to be able to punch the Record button whenever the spirit moves you is truly a rarity for most musicians, and actually living in her own recording studio enabled Tori to capture magical moments that would otherwise have been lost. "Baker Baker" was reportedly recorded early one morning when, upon rising, Tori had declared herself ready. For a songwriter who on occasion composes in record, resulting in an "instant take," the situation was ideal. "Bells For Her" poured out of Tori one day as she sat playing the upright piano; she did not know what she was singing from one word to the next and had to listen to the recording and write the words down afterwards in order to learn them. Luckily Eric was in record. "I have the red button on all the time, even when she is just

going to 'dust' the piano. Inevitably she'll write something when she thinks no one is listening." Tori has often compared the songwriting process to that of giving birth, rationalizing that some babies pop out very quickly while others demand hour upon hour of painstaking labor. She isn't without a helping hand, however, stating, "As a writer, John Lennon has been my biggest influence, my mentor really. He'll come and visit me sometimes."

Tori did leave the desert once during the recording for an unlikely visit to "The Tate House" in Beverly Hills, the site of the Charles Manson murders. She went there to see Trent Reznor of Nine-Inch Nails, the band which warrants a mention in "Precious Things" with the line "*with their NINE-INCH nails and little fascist panties tucked inside the heart of every nice girl.*" Trent was renting the house (which has since been torn down), and he had happily agreed to lend his voice to backup vocals on the track "Past the Mission." Tori did find the place slightly spooky, and as evidence cites her failed attempt to cook the willowy Trent— "who I'd been dying to fatten up"—and company her famous Southern baked chicken, a fail-proof recipe which failed miserably. Upon telephoning her mother, Tori received the explanation that there was probably a "heavy curse" on the kitchen as an heir to the Folger's Coffee empire had "perished" in the house. Despite the eerie atmosphere, Trent laid down some almost unrecognizably smooth vocals. Tori says, "his life is completely committed to being an innovative and experimental musician. I think accomplishing that means more to him than anything except for maybe Maise."

"I don't think people really understood what *Under the Pink* was; *Under the Pink* was an impressionist painting, it wasn't supposed to be diary form like *Little Earthquakes*. The critics would get ahold of it and say, well it's not as intimate as *Little Earthquakes*. It was intimate but it wasn't in diary form, and they didn't understand that it was a conscious choice that I made, to write in a different form. I wrote it like the landscape; you have to crawl into the landscape.

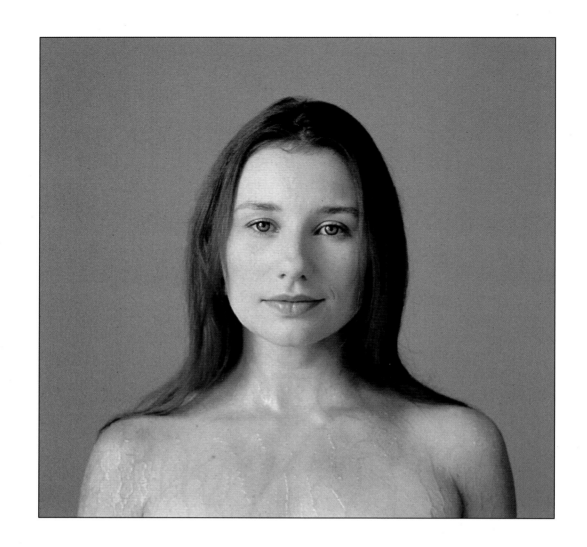

"You cannot understand the smell of the sage and the feel of the dry on your throat unless you feel it, unless you're there, unless you're in the landscape. If you read someone's diary you can live a bit voyeuristically. Well, I didn't want that on this record. You had to be in the middle of the desert, so I wrote it like a painting, and I still think it's misunderstood. It's a very deep work, you have to crawl into it to understand the many, many layers. And I don't think a lot of people know how to access their different layers to go there. Some do."

After dismissing a variety of possible names for the new album, including *God with a Capital G,* Tori settled upon *Under the Pink.* As she revealed to the *Take to the Sky* fanzine: "I felt like I dealt with the Son on the last record and now I'm going after the Father." The title alludes to many concepts for many people, but for Tori it describes what we would find if we stripped off everyone's skin, referring both to the true inner being we all hide, as well as to the fact that we all look the same underneath our fragile covering. Pink is, of course, synonymous with girls, and *Under the Pink* explores what lurks beneath the concept of girl.

"It's definitely an abstract piece of work. It was a conscious choice not to write another diary like *Little Earthquakes.* I'd revealed so much I truly believed anything I revealed in that manner so soon after *Little Earthquakes* wouldn't be enough, and I couldn't put myself under the microscope again so soon. It's like when you're falling in love for the first time—the newness, the getting to know each other—even if they eat onions everything is O.K. I mean, peeing is romantic. The surprise is the romance, the vulnerability. *Little Earthquakes* was the romance phase between me and the listeners. I knew I had to change direction because it was like, 'Yeah, we've already seen you naked; now what do you have? Skinless?' So with *Under the Pink,* I put some clothes on."

With a new album laid down, Tori left the wide-open desert and flew to the crowded madness of London to polish up her new set of "children." In between slews of interviews, Tori was working on launching the first U.K. single,

"Cornflake Girl." The song was to have two different EP releases (true to Tori's usual prolificacy). One would feature three cover versions—tributes to Jimi Hendrix ("If 6 Was 9"), Billie Holiday ("Strange Fruit"), and Joni Mitchell ("A Case of You"). The other would include her own haunting version of "Home on the Range" subtitled the "Cherokee Edition" along with a piano suite. The "Cornflake Girl" video was also in the works.

To further increase the frantic pace of promotion for the new album, it was decided that the first U.S. single would be "God." Tori returned to America in mid December to shoot the video with director Melody McDaniel, also responsible for music videos for the Cranberries and Catherine Wheel. The resulting work was perhaps the strongest statement Tori had made yet about organized religion. In the arresting video Tori sings, *"God sometimes you just don't come through do you need a woman to look after you"* while a multitude of live rats crawl over her body (inspired by a religious ceremony in India) and participates in a ritual involving large snakes practiced by a Fundamentalist religious sect. Tori's father feels that the song is "theologically very sound," but admits to feeling a bit unsettled about the snakes.

The video for "Cornflake Girl" was also shot in Los Angeles at the same time; this was directed by Big TV! (two British men, Andy and Monty), and the haunt- ingly artistic video was adored by European fans. With its warped *Wizard of Oz* plot, the predomi- nantly black and  white video features Tori falling and spinning through space—along with feath- ers, shells, and a burning house—dressed in a tattered white dress and furry eskimo boots. She is weighed down by the piano tied to her foot, but an enor- mous spiderweb catches her fall.

Still from the God *video*

Under the Pink was released in February of 1994 ("I've always been a winter kind of girl"), debuted at number 1 in the U.K. charts and went Gold within one week. Its juxtaposition of musical styles, from the epic, bridge-filled "Yes, Anastasia" to the light-hearted cabaret of "The Wrong Band," leaves no genre unrepresented; jazz, funk, full orchestras, and ancient hymns all find a place on the album. The versatility of Tori's voice is showcased on every track, and brings the personality of each song to life. It is difficult to reconcile the vocals in the wistful beauty of "*Baker Baker baking a cake make me a day make me whole again*" with the driving force of "The Waitress"'s "*But I believe in peace Bitch.*" The U.K. press seemed to have adopted Tori as an honorary citizen, accepting her "weird chick" attributes as emblems of a good old British eccentric. *Q* magazine printed a downright cozy piece on Tori in their February issue, featuring excerpts from her diary and photographs of her cooking toffee apples in her flat and washing her underwear at a local London launderette.

Tori spent the first half of February in America adhering to a feverish promotional schedule, granting press interviews and broadcasting live from radio stations from coast to coast. Appearances on *The Today Show, Entertainment Tonight,* CNN, and *The Tonight Show with Jay Leno* were slotted in along with another visit with MTV. Press interviews were an almost hourly occurrence, and in the next few months articles appeared in all manner of magazines from *US* and *Entertainment Weekly* to the male-oriented *Details* and a rather ground-breaking cover on the March issue of "America's Only Rock 'n' Roll Magazine," *Creem.* She then hopped back across the Atlantic to the U.K. for yet another set of interviews and appearances, including the annual Brit Awards, at which she munched on a banana much to the delight of the music press photographers. The "Brits" weren't just another industry appearance, but turned out to be an opportunity for Tori to meet up with Polly Harvey for the first time and with Björk again. After Björk and Polly's duet cover version of the Stones' "Satisfaction"

Under the Pink *goes Gold*

at the ceremony, Tori, looking for sympathetic company, knocked on their trailer door and said, "Can I come in?" She was duly pulled inside for a mutual admiration session during which the three women confirmed that they were, as Tori says, "soulmates."

Tori began the preliminary segment of her 1994 *Under the Pink* world tour in England's Newcastle Upon Tyne on February 24th. Performing at sold-out venues in major cities throughout England and Scotland for the remainder of February and the first week in March, Tori gave the U.K. a tantalizing taste of her new album.

In March Atlantic Records distributed a promotional CD entitled *Tea with the Waitress*, which features Tori being interviewed by Bob Waugh of Washington D.C.'s WHFS-FM interspersed with segments of songs from *Under the Pink*. Included in this treasure-trove of insight into the songs is Tori's monologue on her concept of God, wonderfully summarized in her disgust at "that concept of sending a son where we as women could, like, breast feed him and give him milk but he's not going to soil his dinky with us, what's that all about? That really bugged me. The whole concept that Jesus was not going to make it with a babe; what—that's going to make him more holy?"

Neil Gaiman continued to turn up, first in the lyrics to "Space Dog" (*where's Neil when you need him*) and again as the writer of the introduction to the *Tori Pink Tour* tour booklet. He was actually returning a favor, as Tori had written the introduction to his November 1993 compilation entitled DEATH: *The High Cost of Living* in which she contemplates the nature and personality of death, noting, "On bad days I talk to Death constantly." Neil is delighted with the affinity between Tori and *Sandman* fans, remarking that "fans of one are normally fans of the other. If you started shooting wildly from the stage at a Tori concert, you'd probably hit a number of people wearing *Sandman* T-shirts or *Death* T-

shirts. The last gig of hers I went to, people kept coming up to me for autographs from the crowd which was really embarrassing."

A hectic week in Japan followed, during which Tori created the storyboard for the U.S. video for "Cornflake Girl" which she directed with Nancy Bennett. The song (inspired by Alice Walker's novel *Possessing the Secret of Joy* wherein the mothers of a tribe allow the removal of their daughters' genitalia as part of a traditional ritual) deals with betrayal amongst women. Feeling that the abstract European video wasn't quite right for her American fans, she put together a gripping visual adaptation of the song. The video follows Tori as she drives a pick-up truck across the desert with what she calls "the girls of tomorrow" in the back. It sounds like a pretty picture, but, as should be expected, there are a few ugly twists including the lassoing of one girl's lovely neck by a  rope attached to another girl's pinky finger. Tori witnesses the whole thing from the rear-view mirror, the observer of two parts of herself, the bully and the bullied. She finally steps on the brake for a lone cowboy who the girls then stick in a pot and cook for dinner. Of this twist she says, "You know if I'm going to have a boy in my video I'm going to be eating him." All in just over five minutes, the song, driven by the lyrics *"this is not really happening you bet your life it is,"* is brought to life in full color.

The "Pretty Good Year" video brought Cindy Palmano's beautiful approach back to Tori's work. The video, which has an unmistakable Palmano air about it, is shot in an almost empty room. A bed, a chair, and a wardrobe are the only props, and Tori enters the room by crashing through a large-paned window. The song, inspired by a letter Tori received from a fan—a boy in England named Greig who was feeling sorry for himself because he just didn't know what women

wanted—holds no pity. There are men in the video; one is asleep on the bed, and others catch Tori as she falls backwards and place her gingerly in the chair. The video closes with Tori exiting the room via a reverse jump out of the window which replaces all of the glass.

The rest of March was spent completing a whirlwind tour of North America, playing to crowds of no more than 1,500 in Seattle; San Francisco; Los Angeles; Chicago; Toronto; Washington, D.C.; Glenside; New York City; Boston; and Atlanta; rounding it up on April 2 in Montreal. It was near-impossible for ticket-holders to gain access to the doors of these concert halls as throngs of fans blockaded the entrances begging for tickets.

A break of a mere two days followed which was primarily spent getting back to Europe in order  to play the Cigalle in Paris on April 5. The night after Kurt Cobain's tragic suicide, Tori opened her show in Berlin with a medley of "American Pie (The Day the Music Died)" and "Smells Like Teen Spirit." Dates in Amsterdam, Zurich, Milan, and Rome followed sandwiched around a week of concerts in Germany. Then it was back to the U.K. to satisfy the growing demand for more Tori. Three consecutive nights playing to a total of over 6,000 fans at the prestigious London Palladium convinced Tori that England had fallen in love with "Cornflake Girl," as the usually hushed audience drowned out the opening of the hit single with their cheers. Tori's mother delights in telling her own cornflake story, set in a London high street. Mrs. Amos and her daughter were strolling along, minding their own business and looking distinctly unfamous when two little girls came screeching up to them shouting, "The cornflake girl! The cornflake girl!" After a quick disappearance, the girls breathlessly returned with their own mother in tow

announcing, "Mum, it's Tori Amos!" Much to her daughters' embarrassment, the mother on the spot enquired politely, "Do I know you?" A single shriek of "the *cornflake* girl, mum!" resulted in a why-didn't-you-say-so brand of instant recognition after which Tori signed autographs for the entire family. Mrs. Amos remembers "Tori turned to me and said, 'But Ma, I'm a raisin girl,' a point very few people seem to get."

May began in Ireland with gigs in Belfast and Dublin. Tori and her crew then made their way to Sweden for a night in Stockholm where Neil Gaiman just happened to be with Alice Cooper; he surprised Tori at her hotel and the two of them "just went off dancing through the streets of Stockholm singing 'Hey Big Spender.'" She then went on to performances in three Dutch cities before returning to Paris on the 10.

The video for "Past the Mission" was shot on location in Spain during the next week. This compelling video follows Tori as she enters a Spanish village with a young girl on either  arm. She becomes a pied piper of sorts, accumulating a following of women as she skips through the narrow streets of the town with boys and men looking on from the rooftops. After a heart-stopping confrontation with a young priest, Tori and her female entourage leave the village confines to exalt in the open fields.

Press coverage had been building up to a crescendo, and in May Tori was featured on the covers of both of England's top music magazines, *Q* and *Vox*. *Q*, with its arresting photo of Tori, Björk, and PJ Harvey on the cover, contained a wonderfully convoluted simultaneous interview with the three magical musicians during which Tori asserted, "We have tits. We have three holes. That's what we have in common." It was Tori's idea to play on Marky Mark's Calvin Klein ads on the *VOX* cover and dress up in a pair of men's briefs; the photo is rather sweetly captioned by Tori with, "I'm the Queen of the Nerds."

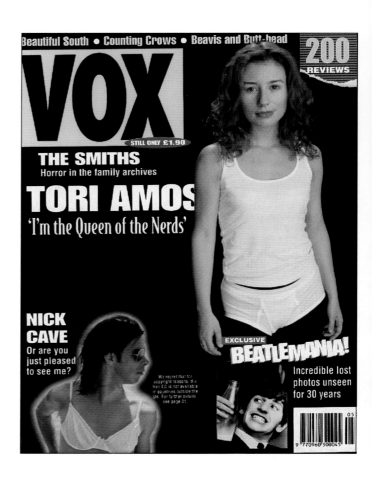

Tori with fellow honoree Marlo Thomas at the Visionary Award ceremony

Governor's citation award

On June 2, 1994, the D.C. Rape Crisis Center presented Tori with a Visionary Award for her "significant work that brings us closer to a world free from all forms of oppression and sexual violence." It was the first time that a recording artist had been given the award, which is presented yearly to "individuals or organizations who have made an outstanding contribution toward the promotion of social justice." The Center cited "Me and a Gun" as a song which furthered society's awareness of rape. Tori attended the Washington, D.C. ceremony where she announced her founding of the R.A.I.N.N. (Rape, Abuse, and Incest National Network) telephone hotline with the toll-free number of 1-800-656-HOPE. Tori, by singing "Me and a Gun" to audiences night after night, expresses the concept that rape is not something that is quickly overcome—that the healing process is ongoing. In a R.A.I.N.N. flyer she says that she sings the song "as a way of healing the place inside myself that has been hurt, enraged, and numbed by violence." In an achingly open interview in the February 1994 issue of Ireland's *Hot Press* magazine, Tori described the terror and violence she experienced the night of the rape, asserting that "people out there must be told about the self-loathing that follows rape and how it's the greatest breakage in divine law to mutilate themselves, as I have done." Tori's struggle to become "whole again" is addressed throughout the songs on *Under the Pink*; she comes to terms with her own emotional unavailability since the rape in "Baker Baker," and acknowledges her own violence in "The Waitress." Helping herself and others to stop seeing themselves as victims is absolutely vital to Tori.

Tori teamed up with her old friend Sandra Bernhard again in the June issue of *Interview.* Tori herself had been interviewed for the magazine in May of 1992, but this time it was Tori's turn to ask the questions (at the request of Miss Bernhard). The interview takes off as an informal conversation about, among many other things, crystal suppositories, self-hatred, and peanut butter and

Tori with Mom and Dad at Dr. Amos's retirement reception, June '94

jelly. The two have known each other for years; in fact, Tori's not-yet-famous voice can be found singing backup vocals on Sandra's cover version of Prince's "Little Red Corvette" on her 1989 *Without You I'm Nothing* record.

A caricature, photos of Tori at the age of two, fifteen, and thirty, and an article entitled "The Power and the Passion" appeared in the June 30 issue of *Rolling Stone*, the rock bible that named "Silent All These Years" as number 98 in its Top 100 videos of all time and elected Tori "Best New Female Singer" in 1993. Of touring, Tori says, "I live for it. It's my lifeblood." The official U.S. tour was now underway. In order to satisfy the huge demand for tickets while still remaining faithful to the idea of intimate shows, Tori scheduled multiple nights in larger cities, playing two or three nights in a row at New York City's Beacon Theatre; the Warner Theatre in Washington, D.C.; and Detroit's State Theatre in June. She also managed to play two shows in one night at a few select venues. There never seemed to be enough tickets, but Tori and her management felt that to play in larger halls would not suit her performance nor, ultimately, her fans. Tori was, however, worried about not having enough time to spare for her fans with such a demanding tour schedule. Neil Gaiman remembers receiving a phone call from Tori; "She was saying she didn't know what to do because up until now she'd always stayed after every gig and hugged everybody… I wound up giving her this lecture which I've later been told a number of other people had given her… I said, 'Look, they haven't bought a ticket to hug you. What are you going to do when you play Wembley Stadium—hug 60,000 people?' Obviously she's touched their lives; she's become part of them. But she has to move away in order to get to the next city in time."

The 1994 *Under the Pink* tour retained all of the best aspects of the 1992 *Little Earthquakes* tour while taking on a few enhancements. Aside from a wealth of wonderful new songs in attendance at the "dinner party," as Tori likes to describe a concert, there were a few more "guests" along for the ride. Concert-goers kept

Dr. Amos joins Tori, Arthur Spivak, and the crew for a well-earned dinner

TORI AMOS
UNDER THE PINK / FALL TOUR '94
NOT LONG NOW....

their ears open for covers of Led Zeppelin's "Whole Lotta Love," "Bad Company," "Landslide" by Steve Nicks, Bruce Springsteen's "I'm On Fire," or the aching standard "When Sonny Gets Blue." Anything could show up.

Most importantly, this time Tori brought a nine-foot Bösendorfer grand piano on the road with her. She now had the "best piano in the world" as her faithful companion each night. Keeping the "Bösey" company onstage, and serving perhaps as a reminder of the little girl within, is the upright "Bells for Her" piano which has toys hidden inside it, and some naughty ones at that. "Trolls have always been her favorite," Mrs. Amos says, "she loved those ugly little creatures since she was wee, tearing the heads off her sister's Barbies to feed her little dears." Tori now works with two Bösendorfers, "the one that I own and the one that I tour with. The Bösey I own is very much a recording instrument, she's not into touring. She's eight years old now. She was in a church in New York City for a while where she got battered and abused, and she got shoved around to every club in the city before she was in the church, so she just got the shit beat out of her in New York, and I felt like she and I understood each other, so, she had to be rebuilt kind of, and I just take really good care of her. She gathers her energy and then we put it into the record. The piano I'm touring with is a year old, so she's feisty and wants to see the world and check out boys multiculturally. She was rotting in this showroom in London. So she's happy to be on the road with me, meeting all these cute dudes."

A road crew made up of fourteen people was now following (and oftentimes preceding) Tori across America in a tour bus. Also along for the ride on this tour was a Native American singer by the name of Bill Miller who grew up on a Mohican Indian reservation. Tori herself chose Bill as an opening act, and asked him to remain with her throughout the U.S. tour rather than picking up various different acts as she had during 1992. Bill's music and his attitude toward life seemed to share a common thread with Tori's, and he never failed to set the tone for the evening.

Another added touch on the 1994 tour was the lighting. John Witherspoon says, "I knew this was coming up and we [John and Simon Sidi, the lighting designer] sat and discussed one person sitting at the piano—how can we light it and make it interesting without being distracting? These particular lights called the Icon we had used on World Party; they're a computerized moving light which can change color, and they're a beautiful light… everyone's commented how it just adds to the show." Tori also chose to play piano with the use of loops for both "God" and "Cornflake Girl."

With these few, carefully chosen changes, Tori continued to present pure music stripped of synthetic decoration. It was just a girl and a piano out on the stage, baring her soul to crowds of strangers each night. Her ability to express anguish, confusion, and pain, along with joy, sexuality, and her own brand of witchy humor all within two hours is truly a roller-coaster ride. To carry the audience along on the journey is next to impossible, but she does it, and when the concert is over, not one member of the crowd seems ready to float back down to earth.

In order to combat the many bootleg CDs circulating, Tori decided to record many of her shows, giving her an arsenal of live material to choose from for a possible live album release. Unhappy about her fans spending money on poor-quality recordings, Tori felt a bit better when Robert Plant advised her that "you ain't nothing until you're bootlegged."

Tori's manager of five years, Arthur Spivak, says that "the hysteria for what Tori is doing is spreading because there are more people emotionally attaching themselves to it. I think it geometrically progresses. The reason why we decided to do what we've done—which is to build very, very slowly and very patiently—is because we always felt that as people saw her in the most intimate places possible that the energy would just continue to go from one person to ten people to one hundred people." John Witherspoon says simply, "Hate her or love her;

Tori, Eric Rosse, and Arthur Spivak

October 1994 SPIN *Magazine cover*

it's a great show." Arthur's feeling is that the 1994 *Under the Pink* tour "seems to be definitely taking on a life of its own, which is good because she is definitely touching people in a very, very deep, deep way." Noting that shows in the past would sell out immediately as all the tickets were snapped up by die-hard fans, now with multiple nights and slightly larger venues "more people are getting a chance to see her and to spread the word. I think that's where it is, I think there's almost like a nuclear reaction." Arthur, who has worked with the likes of the Smithereens, Little Steven, Midnight Oil, and Peter Cetera, and who has been actor/comedian Paul Reiser's manager for the past eleven years, was as instantly enamored with Tori as everyone else who meets her for the first time seems to be. Recalling their introduction, he says "Tori and I connected very, very quickly… she sent me a tape with a little Tori-ism on it, so I listened to the tape and I just fell in love with it… she's just such a funny human being, she's totally irreverent, totally unique—they got rid of the cookie cutter when she came out."

On July 25, Tori played at the Meyerhof Hall in Baltimore, and the audience was sprinkled with more than a few professors and students from the Peabody Conservatory. During her customary chat with the audience Tori reportedly burst out with, "Hey! The folks from Peabody are here. That's cool. They've got a new motto round Peabody these days: 'If we kick you out, you can make it.'" After the show Peabody Director Robert Pierce and state delegate Jennie Forehand appeared backstage to present Tori with a Governor's Citation from the state of Maryland for her founding of the sexual assault hotline.

Tori spent the month of August playing to crowds in Florida, Georgia, Tennessee, Louisiana, Texas, Oklahoma, New Mexico, Arizona, and Nevada. REM's Michael Stipe made his way over from Athens to attend one of the Atlanta shows, and he and Tori had an interesting dinner afterward during which the two serenaded the other diners in the restaurant with a rendition of "The Star-Spangled Banner."

"We were proving to the geniuses at our table that the 'Star-Spangled Banner' isn't even two octaves, much less four as someone had claimed," Tori says, adding, "It's a wonder Michael and I ever get anything done, because he's absolutely the best playmate you could ever want."

Tori also played in front of the rest of the nation with another appearance on *The Tonight Show with Jay Leno,* unabashedly bringing the subject of masturbation to Middle America's attention with her performance of "Icicle" (*and when my hand touches myself I can finally rest my head and when they say 'take of his body,' I think I'll take from mine instead*).

Three straight sold-out nights playing a sort of homecoming in the city that hosted her rock-chick days at Los Angeles' 2,700 seat Pantages Theatre followed, where fans and press created a furor. As always, Eddie Van Halen showed up in L.A., and Tori says that the feeling that it gave her "really can't be equaled, except by Jimmy Page. I think the guitar players understand because I steal from them so much." An hour on AM Radio with prestigious Los Angeles host Michael Jackson proved to be yet another milestone for Tori. The twenty-five-year veteran disc jockey who has interviewed Gorbachev, several U.S. presidents (and "everyone that has been on this planet that has been meaningful" according to Arthur Spivak) was reportedly "blown away" by Tori. On her way out of the studio, Tori was greeted by the next guest, director of the C.I.A. Admiral Woolsey, who stopped her to say that he just wanted her to know that his son is a huge fan. She replied, "I think I want your job."

A dramatic shot of Tori, wearing only blood-red lipstick, brought the October cover of SPIN to life. The article entitled "Sex, God, & Rock 'n' Roll" ensures that any reader of the new music bible that SPIN has become who didn't know Tori Amos before won't forget her in a hurry. She says, "I happen to adore red lipstick. It just gets on everything, so I usually only wear it when I do laundry bare-assed."

The *Under the Pink* tour, just a girl and a piano on stages around the world, wound up its eleventh month in Australia in mid December. By presenting herself just as she is, Tori gained a following as diverse as it is devoted. "I think she is having a positive and important effect on this generation," says Arthur Spivak. Tori says, "I am inspired constantly by the kids that come to the shows. They give me new vision just by showing their true selves. If I can inspire them to be their own saviors, then I've done a good thing."

Collaborations and covers filled the tiny gaps between shows and gave Tori the chance to change the frequency of her creative outpourings. A duet with Michael Stipe, entitled "It Might Hurt a Little Bit," was originally intended for the Johnny Depp film *Don Juan de Marco*, but was shelved indefinitely once Tori and Michael discovered that the soundtrack, initially slated to feature "alternative" music became a wee bit too M.O.R. for their tastes. It seems that Bryan Adams, contrary to *Billboard* belief, may not be everyone's cup of tea. Moving from one male musical icon to the next, Tori recorded another duet, this time with Tom Jones; "I Wanna Get Back with You" appears on Jones's *The Lead and How to Swing It* album. "Party Man," a song co-written by Tori and Peter Gabriel, appears on the *Virtuosity* soundtrack, and the *Higher Learning* soundtrack features an original, "Butterfly," along with a cover of R.E.M.'s "Losing My Religion." Tori recorded a cover version of "Famous Blue Raincoat" for the Leonard Cohen tribute album *Tower of Song*. She topped the list off rather nicely with a duet with her idol and major musical influence Robert Plant contained on the Led Zeppelin tribute album *Encomium* in the form of an eight-minute version of "Down by the Seaside."

In the meantime, the *Earthquake* and *Pink* girls were soon to sit down to dinner with some new party guests. As Tori warned, "I'm starting to write again. I don't know what my next work's going to be, but I think there's going to be a lot of bloodletting on it."

BOYS FOR PELE

(1995 – 1996)

The underlying current on *Boys for Pele*—an album named for the Hawaiian volcano goddess of destruction and creation who, as legend has it, commanded the sacrifice of young boys—is one of self-recognition and empowerment. The eighteen songs on the album came to Tori as she attempted to come to terms with her separation from Eric Rosse. She says, "It's affected everything I've written. He's given me some amazing gifts and amazing ways to look at life. And I'm trying to carry them with me."

The album represents an expedition of self-discovery, not as a musician or as a lover, but as a human being. According to Tori, "It was a journey in me finding my own fire—my own flame—not through another person or through things, or through the piano even, but just trying to find it as a person. I had to find fragments  that sort of made up more of the whole. This record really took me to some of the hidden places in my heart as a woman. The programs that I have carried with me started to break down. The way I look at life changed with this record." Tori admits that facing up to the boys on this album was "a bit of an eye-opener," and she realized that she could, and had to, find her own passion rather than stealing it from the men in her life.

Tori recognized that it is sometimes necessary to go to war and come face to face with some of the more terrifying aspects of life in order to restore the balance. The girls on *Boys* forge unabashedly into dark, dense, and cold forests; humid, tangled jungles; as well as newly cultivated farmers' fields. The violently up-front fury of "Professional Widow" (*give me peace, love, and a*

hard cock) must be confronted, just as the heartbroken plea within "Hey Jupiter" (*nothing's been the same so are you gay are you blue thought we both could use a friend to run to*) had to be laid bare.

And what better place to "reel the girls in" than an old church in Ireland? The physical manifestation of an institution that had so influenced her both mentally and spiritually throughout her life turned out to be the perfect setting for the fragment-gathering Tori had to undertake. Tori's penchant for recording "on location" took on new meaning as she and her crew descended upon the church in Delgany for six weeks in July and August of 1995. Astonishingly enough, Tori, not known for the ease of her relationship with organized religion, found the Reverend David Muir "really quite magical" and the congregation "open and wonderful to us." Tori maintains that she and her crew "used the church basically as an instrument because we had mikes in the church. You could say that the ambiance of the church became another instrument."

The freedom inherent in recording without the time pressures of a studio was, as always, imperative to Tori's unique songwriting process. As Alan Friedman, the programmer on *Boys for Pele*, says, "She records very much out of a flow of consciousness." Another unusual element was Tori's decision to use her live crew to record the album. Mark Hawley and Marcel Van Limbeek, the sound engineers who worked with Tori on the *Under the Pink* tour, conspired to capture on tape the direct emotional impact they transmit in the live performance arena. Depending upon which song Tori felt ready to record at any given time (usually divulged with the announcement "here's who's coming today"), technical preparations necessary for that "girl" would be made. Much inventive spirit and a complete lack of the usual can't-be-done studio attitude prevailed. Alan recalls the time in Delgany as "a completely freeing experience within the record making process. There's

usually a certain protocol when people make records, and that was completely thrown out the window on this record, which was brilliant."

In order to capture Tori's sound, a box was constructed to house a harpsichord, the keyboard of her Bösendorfer (the remainder of the piano was on the outside of the box), a piano stool, a little lamp, and, of course, Tori. Of being "completely enclosed in a box," Tori says, "sometimes I wonder if they did it for revenge. I was waiting for them to just carve out two inches in the bottom and pass me some spaghetti underneath."

Tori's move outward from the piano to the harpsichord, "the bloodline of the piano," lends *Boys for Pele* an at once completely new and bygone air. Tori, who spent months on a piano stool, a Bösendorfer on her right side and a harpsichord on her left, cannot overemphasize the importance of the ancient instrument. "It's just made the whole concept of keyboards make more sense to me. I wanted to capture the gut, the heart, and the soul of the instrument—its depth."

A befittingly unusual harem of other voices and musical frequencies ended up joining Tori, her Bösey, and her harpsichord on the album. Playing the harmonium and the clavichord in addition to the harpsichord gave Tori a group of instruments she refers to as "the real cats, the fifteenth fucking century people—no pop stars." The mournfully beautiful sound of the Black Dyke Mills Band, a brass band made up of miners; a gospel choir; the London Sinfonia; the inimitable George Porter, Jr., on bass; and Steve Caton, longtime friend and musical collaborator on "all manner of guitars," only begins a list that becomes increasingly diverse the deeper you dig. The very first sound to be heard on *Boys for Pele* is a Leslie cabinet set up outside the church in the graveyard. A Marshall amp and a local group of amateur bagpipers also make appearances. Perhaps the oddest guest is the bull who lived at the farm next door to the church. During the recording, it soon became apparent that the bull, whose incredible bellows could be heard every night, simply had to be part of "Professional Widow" (he is duly

Inside "the box"

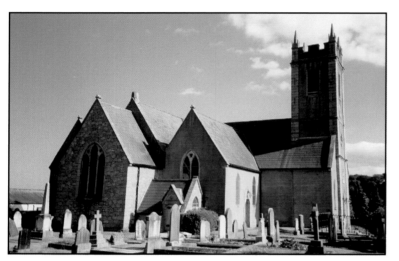

The church in Delgany, Ireland

Under the hood of the Bösey

credited). After Mark and Marcel spent several hours waiting for the bull—who awkwardly chose that very afternoon to display his shy nature—to "speak" for the microphones they had set up in the farmer's field, they ended up capturing more than they had bargained for on tape. Hence the unprecedented sampling of the genuine sound of a farmer shoveling bullshit making its way on to a major-label record release as part of the rhythm loop of "Widow."

Tori and her crew left the church to move on to a "wonderfully damp Georgian house" in County Cork, Ireland, to record for another month or so and then jumped into the voodoo-rich environment of New Orleans for the final mixing. As Tori recalls, "Everything started to become sort of a map. Where was the frequency of the music—what needed to get on tape geographically?" She originally planned to record the entire album in the American South, but "every cell pointed me in the direction of Ireland, and Ireland really made up one of the elements of the South that I grew up with—that energy—and the force that the church had." She chose to complete the recording process in Louisiana because "North Carolina is nothing like what I remember. There aren't the smells and the tastes and the frequency. New Orleans represented a certain melting pot to me of tastes, and darkness as well as joyousness, and I wanted to work from both perspectives."

The cover and all of the artwork for *Boys for Pele*—once again shot by Cindy Palmano who continues to visually capture the essence of Tori's work—was photographed in Louisiana as well. Truly "Southern" imagery—porches, rifles, chickens, and pigs—intermeshes with less immediate and more surreal scenes, the most arresting of which is never pictured in full: Tori standing beside a flaming piano in the middle of a gas station parking lot surrounded by fire engines and bystanders.

The video for the album's first single, "Caught a Lite Sneeze," carried on the dreamlike, almost hallucinatory quality inherent in the album's artwork. Directed by Mike Liscombe, who was given full creative license from Tori, the video is rich, multi-layered, and, according to Liscombe, "open to many interpretations."  He feels that it represents "a sur- real spiritual jour- ney" and "the process of finding inner peace with oneself." Tori says that Liscombe "wanted to take the video into a place that brings together the fight of the soul with the fight of the physical self." This concept manifests itself in recurring sequences of multiple Toris pushing, pulling, and being swept along with another Tori seated in a white armchair that is sliding back and forth along a leaf-strewn wooden floor. The field of vision twists and turns, rotating to show alternately the inside of the room and a vast expanse of water that ends in a waterfall. The cyclical nature of the song itself is perfectly suited to the rhythm of the video which *Billboard* magazine called "strange," "complicated," and "visually stunning."

The second video, "Talula," is an abrupt departure from the hypnotic nature of the "Sneeze" video but retains the feeling of an alternate reality. Shot in a deserted power plant, it was directed by Mark Kohr, known for his work with the likes of Primus, Green Day, and Alanis Morissette. Featuring a blowtorch wielding Tori along with a variety of other characters including tightrope walkers and laboratory assistants, the video's theme, according to Tori, is "the process of dehumanization."

Boys for Pele received quite a mixture of reviews and reactions, while seeming to cement Tori's reputation as a truly unique, unpredictable, and ever-evolving talent. The January 23, 1996, release debuted at number 2 on the

Billboard charts in the United States and at number 1 in the U.K. It was given only two stars by *Rolling Stone*, who criticized Tori's "enigmatic artifice and fanciful metaphors." As tradition has had it, the Brits seemed once again more open to Tori's brand of music; *Q* magazine declared, "Free of all creative constraints by the world-spanning successes of her previous works, this is surely the sound of Tori Amos the way she wants to sound" and awarded the album four stars. A very young, pale, minimalist image of Tori graced the cover of the March 1996 issue of *Spin*, while an altogether different Tori—glamorous and sophisticated to the point of Sophia Loren resemblance—could be found on *Musician* magazine's May cover. Uncertainty on the media's part as to how to categorize Tori's music did not, however, daunt journalists when faced with the task of summing up her persona; her standing as pop music's reigning queen of mad-as-a-hatterdom remained unchallenged. Headlines such as "Deep Space Tori" (New York's *Village Voice*), "Too Many Kooks?" (London's *Observer*), "Ginger Nut" (*TimeOut*), and "Twisted" (*Q*) prevailed. "I am garlic personified," says Tori. "You know, garlic and extra virgin olive oil. Garlic is garlic. You don't want it in ice cream, but you definitely want it when there are vampires around."

The Dew Drop Inn Tour began on February 23 in Ipswich, England. A few dates in Scotland followed before Tori sunk her teeth in and filled the month of March with twenty-two shows in seven European countries (including "one of my favorite shows, Florence—primarily because I was kind of having the hots for Michelangelo and it was just turning me on") before commencing her U.S. tour in Tampa, Florida on April 9. Tori, her Bösendorfer, and the now indispensable harpsichord were joined by another musical voice in the form of Steve Caton on guitar with whom Tori says she was able to "keep the intimacy and free-form within the show while adding a new flavor." As

she says, "I'm not ready for marriage: no band." As *The Guardian* asks in its review of her Edinburgh, Scotland show, "Who needs a rhythm section when you have a left hand like hers?" Two sold-out nights at London's Royal Albert Hall ended in standing ovations, and the *Evening Standard*'s Max Bell described the concert as "undiluted vicarious pleasure."

Tori feels that she has "never been so present" as she is on this tour. Declaring the tour itself to be "the next record," she insists that "the readings of the songs completely change when they're next to each other. Now, when I sandwich a song from *Little Earthquakes* in between two of the *Pele* girls they all enrich each other—they dance with each other and they have a glass of chardonnay with each other." And so the tour goes; Tori living purely in the present, insisting that, "I with every cell want to be *here*, because this isn't something you can take home with you in your hand." But it's a certainty that a new group of girls has already begun knocking at the door, and that Tori can look forward to a lifetime of creativity and passion.

TOUR ITINERARY

1992 LITTLE EARTHQUAKES TOUR

January
29 **Shaw Theatre**, *London, England*
30 **Shaw Theatre**, *London, England*

February
7   **Blue Coat Arts Centre**, *Liverpool, England*
8   **Arts Centre**, *Hanley, England*
9   **University**, *Reading, England*
11 **Arena**, *Middleboro, England*
13 **King Tut's**, *Glasgow, Scotland*
14 **Music Box**, *Edinburgh, Scotland*
15 **River Side**, *Newcastle, England*
16 **Polytechnic**, *Nottingham, England*
17 **University**, *Manchester, England*
19 **Arts Centre**, *Norwich, England*
20 **Spring St. Theatre**, *Hull, England*
21 **University**, *Sheffield, England*

March
7   **Opera House**, *Frankfurt, Germany*
9   **Kaffe Giesing**, *Munich, Germany*
10 **Floz**, *Berlin, Germany*
11 **Market Hall**, *Hamburg, Germany*
15 **Roxy**, *Amsterdam, Holland*
16 **Dal Big Mama**, *Rome, Italy*

April
2   **London Royalty Theatre**, *London, England*
3   **London Royalty Theatre**, *London, England*
5   **Corn Exchange**, *Cambridge, England*
7   **Queen's Hall**, *Edinburgh, Scotland*
10 **Free Trade Hall**, *Manchester, England*
11 **Town Hall**, *Birmingham, England*
20 **Bottom Line**, *New York City, USA*
21 **Industry**, *Pontiac, Michigan USA*
22 **Birchmere**, *Alexandria, Virginia USA*
23 **St. Andrew's**, *Detroit, Michigan USA*
24 **Theatre of Living Arts**, *Philadelphia, PA USA*
25 **Rivoli's**, *Toronto, Ontario Canada*
27 **Iron Horse Music Hall**, *Northampton, Massachusetts USA*
28 **Night Stage**, *Cambridge, Massachusetts USA*
29 **Schubas**, *Chicago, Illinois USA*
30 **Deep Ellum Live**, *Dallas, Texas USA*

May
1   **Rockefeller**, *Houston, Texas USA*
3   **Fine Line Music Cafe**, *Minneapolis, Minnesota USA*
4   **The Point**, *Atlanta, Georgia USA*
6   **Backstage**, *Seattle, Washington USA*
7   **Cultural Center**, *Vancouver, British Columbia Canada*
8   **The Garage**, *Denver, Colorado USA*
9   **Bimbo's**, *San Francisco, California USA*
10 **Sound FX**, *San Diego, California USA*
11 **The Roxy**, *Los Angeles, California USA*
23 **Brash's**, *Melbourne, Australia*
25 **Rose, Shamrock & Thistle**, *Sydney, Australia*
30 **Pablo**, *Taipei, Taiwan*

June
6   **Rock am Ring**, *Hockenheim, Germany*
7   **Alte Oper**, *Frankfurt, Germany*
8   **Stadpark**, *Hamburg, Germany*
9   **Schillersaal**, *Stuttgart, Germany*
10 **Ancienne Belgique**, *Brussels, Belgium*
14 **Night Town**, *Rotterdam, Holland*
28 **Susan Dalal Auditorium**, *Tel Aviv, Isreal*

July
23 **Hotel Borg**, *Reykjavik, Iceland*
24 **Hotel Borg**, *Reykjavik, Iceland*
30 **Phoenix Hill Tavern**, *Louisville, Kentucky USA*
31 **Park West**, *Chicago, Illinois USA*

August
1   **1st Avenue**, *Minneapolis, Minnesota USA*
3   **Club Eastbrook**, *Grand Rapids, Michigan USA*
4   **Peabody's Down Under**, *Cleveland, Ohio USA*
5   **Bogart's**, *Cincinnati, Ohio USA*
6   **Rosebud**, *Pittsburgh, Pennsylvania USA*
7   **Newport Music Hall**, *Columbus, Ohio USA*
9   **The Vogue**, *Indianapolis, Indiana USA*
10 **City Market**, *Indianapolis, Indiana USA*
10 **Jake's**, *Bloomington, Indiana USA*
11 **328 Performance Hall**, *Nashville, Tennessee USA*
12 **Center Stage**, *Atlanta, Georgia USA*
14 **Club Carousel**, *Jacksonville, Florida USA*
15 **State Theatre**, *Tampa, Florida USA*
16 **Carefree Theatre**, *West Palm Beach, Florida USA*
17 **Beacham Theatre**, *Orlando, Florida USA*
22 **Henry Fonda Theatre**, *Los Angeles, California USA*
23 **Henry Fonda Theatre**, *Los Angeles, California USA*
24 **Henry Fonda Theatre**, *Los Angeles, California USA*
25 **Anaconda Theatre**, *Santa Barbara, California USA*
26 **Mandeville Auditorium**, *San Diego, California USA*
28 **Roseland Theatre**, *Portland, Oregon USA*
29 **Moore Theatre**, *Seattle, Washington USA*
30 **WOW Hall**, *Eugene, Oregon USA*

September

1	**Murphy Park Amphitheatre**, *Salt Lake City, Utah USA*
2	**Palace of Fine Arts**, *San Francisco, California USA*
3	**Crest Theatre**, *Sacramento, California USA*
4	**The Coach House**, *San Juan Capistrano, California USA*
5	**The Coach House**, *San Juan Capistrano, California USA*
11	**Storyville**, *New Orleans, Louisiana USA*
12	**The Lumberyard**, *Mobile, Alabama USA*
13	**Lisner Auditorium**, *Washington, DC*
14	**Flood Zone**, *Richmond, Virginia USA*
16	**Dodd Auditorium**, *Fredricksburg, Virginia USA*
17	**Cabell Hall**, *Charlottesville, Virginia USA*
18	**Boathouse**, *Norfolk, Virginia USA*
19	**Rialto Theatre**, *Raleigh, North Carolina USA*
20	**Cultural Center Auditorium**, *Charleston, West Virginia USA*
22	**Bijou Theatre**, *Knoxville, Tennessee USA*
24	**Fine Arts Auditorium**, *Athens, Georgia USA*
25	**The Varsity**, *Baton Rouge, Louisiana USA*
26	**Tower Theatre**, *Houston, Texas USA*
28	**Kimo Theatre**, *Albuquerque, New Mexico USA*
29	**Boulder Theatre**, *Boulder, Colorado USA*
30	**Valley Art Theatre**, *Phoenix, Arizona USA*

October

1	**Valley Art Theatre**, *Phoenix, Arizona USA*
3	**Terrace Ballroom**, *Austin, Texas USA*
5	**Sooner Theatre**, *Norman, Oklahoma USA*
6	**Mississippi Nights**, *St. Louis, Missouri USA*
8	**Town Hall**, *New York City USA*
9	**Town Hall**, *New York City USA*
11	**Count Basie Theatre**, *Red Bank, New Jersey USA*
12	**Town Hall**, *New York City USA*

18	**Berklee Performance Center**, *Boston, Massachusetts USA*
20	**Keswick Theatre**, *Glenside, Pennsylvania USA*
21	**Keswick Theatre**, *Glenside, Pennsylvania USA*
23	**Rockwell Hall**, *Buffalo, New York USA*
25	**Buckley Recital Hall**, *Amherst, Massachusetts USA*
27	**The Penguin**, *Ottawa, Ontario Canada*
28	**Phoenix Concert Theatre**, *Toronto, Ontario Canada*
29	**Cafe Campus**, *Montreal, Quebec Canada*
30	**St. Andrew's Hall**, *Detroit, Michigan USA*

November

1	**Cook College**, *New Brunswick, New Jersey USA*
2	**Shooters Live**, *Cleveland, Ohio USA*
3	**State Theatre**, *Kalamazoo, Michigan USA*
5	**Weasler Auditorium**, *Milwaukee, Wisconsin USA*
6	**Performing Arts Center**, *Purchase, New York USA*
8	**Page Hall**, *Albany, New York USA*
9	**Toad's Place**, *New Haven, Connecticut USA*
10	**Tuxedo Junction**, *Danbury, Connecticut USA*
11	**Steeltown**, *Baltimore, Maryland USA*
12	**Steeltown**, *Baltimore, Maryland USA*
14	**Boutelle Music Hall**, *DeKalb, Illinois USA*
15	**Barrymore Theatre**, *Madison, Wisconsin USA*
16	**McCormick Auditorium**, *Evanston, Illinois*
21	**The Octagon**, *Perth, Australia*
22	**Athenaeum Theatre**, *Melbourne, Australia*
23	**Athenaeum Theatre**, *Melbourne, Australia*
25	**York Theatre**, *Sydney, Australia*
26	**York Theatre**, *Sydney, Australia*
27	**York Theatre**, *Sydney, Australia*
30	**Town Hall**, *Auckland, New Zealand*

1994 UNDER THE PINK TOUR

February

24	**Upon Tyne Theatre**, *Newcastle, England*
25	**Arts Centre**, *Warwick, England*
27	**Pavilion**, *Glasgow, Scotland*
28	**Queenshall**, *Edinburgh, Scotland*

March

1	**Free Trade Hall**, *Manchester, England*
3	**City Varieties Music Hall**, *Leeds, England*
4	**Corn Exchange**, *Cambridge, England*
6	**Her Majesty's Theatre**, *London, England*
7	**Colston Hall**, *Bristol, England*
20	**Meany Hall, U. of Washington**, *Seattle, Washington USA*
21	**Herbst Theatre**, *San Francisco, California USA*
22	**Wadsworth Theatre**, *Los Angeles, California USA*
24	**Vic Theatre**, *Chicago, Illinois USA*
26	**Convocation Hall**, *Toronto, Ontario Canada*
27	**Lisner Auditorium**, *Washington DC*
28	**Keswick Theatre**, *Glenside, Pennsylvania USA*
30	**Symphony Space**, *New York City USA*
31	**The Sanders Theatre**, *Boston, Massachusetts USA*

April

1	**Center Stage**, *Atlanta, Georgia USA*
2	**Theatre L'Olympia**, *Montreal, Quebec Canada*
5	**The Cigalle**, *Paris, France*
6	**Passage 44**, *Brussels, Belgium*
7	**Paradiso**, *Amsterdam, Holland*
9	**Trinitatiskrine**, *Berlin, Germany*
10	**CCH2**, *Hamburg, Germany*
12	**Mozartsaal**, *Frankfurt, Germany*
13	**Schumann Saal**, *Dusseldorf, Germany*
14	**Kleine Liedehalle**, *Stuttgart, Germany*
15	**Prinz Regent**, *Munich, Germany*
17	**Tonhalle**, *Zurich, Switzerland*
18	**Nacionalle**, *Milan, Italy*
19	**Palladium**, *Rome, Italy*
21	**Guildhall**, *Portsmouth, England*
22	**Royal Centre**, *Nottingham, England*
23	**Regent**, *Ipswich, England*
24	**Barbican**, *York, England*
26	**St. Davids Hall**, *Cardiff, Wales*
28	**Palladium**, *London, England*

29 **Palladium,** *London, England*
30 **Palladium,** *London, England*

May
2 **Civic Hall,** *Wolverhampton, England*
3 **Church House,** *Belfast, Ireland*
4 **Olympia,** *Dublin, Ireland*
5 **Cirkus,** *Stockholm, Sweden*
7 **Mecc Conf. Center,** *Maastricht, Holland*
8 **Vereeniging,** *Nijmegen, Holland*
9 **Irkus Theater,** *Scheveninger, Holland*

June
7 **Tiles Center, CW Post College,** *Brookville, New York USA*
8 **Paramount Center for the Arts,** *Peekskill, New York USA*
9 **Bismark Theatre,** *Chicago, Illinois USA*
10 **Theatre on the Ridge,** *Rochester, New York USA*
11 **Orpheum Theatre,** *Boston, Massachusetts USA*
13 **Palace PAC,** *New Haven, Connecticut USA*
15 **Beacon Theatre,** *New York City USA*
16 **Beacon Theatre,** *New York City USA*
17 **State Theatre,** *New Brunswick, New Jersey USA*
18 **Tower Theatre,** *Upper Darby, Pennsylvania USA*
20 **Warner Theatre,** *Washington DC*
21 **Warner Theatre,** *Washington DC*
22 **Warner Theatre,** *Washington DC*
24 **The Strand,** *Providence, Rhode Island USA*
25 **State Theatre,** *Portland, Maine USA*
26 **Flynn Theatre,** *Burlington, Vermont USA*
27 **Palace Theatre,** *Albany, New York USA*
29 **Landmark Theatre,** *Syracuse, New York USA*
30 **Riviera Theatre,** *Buffalo, New York USA*

July
1 **Fulton Theater,** *Pittsburgh, Pennsylvania USA*
2 **State Theatre,** *Detroit, Michigan USA*
4 **State Theatre,** *Detroit, Michigan USA*
5 **Palace Theatre,** *Columbus, Ohio USA*
6 **DeVos Hall,** *Grand Rapids, Michigan USA*
7 **Cleveland Music Hall,** *Cleveland, Ohio USA*
9 **Bismark Theatre,** *Chicago, Illinois USA*
11 **Barrymore Theatre,** *Madison, Wisconsin USA*
12 **Pabst Theatre,** *Milwaukee, Wisconsin USA*
13 **Paramount Theatre,** *Cedar Rapids, Iowa USA*
14 **State Theatre,** *Minneapolis, Minnesota USA*
16 **Murat Theatre,** *Indianapolis, Indiana USA*
17 **Macauley Theatre,** *Louisville, Kentucky USA*
18 **American Theatre,** *St. Louis, Missouri USA*
19 **Midland Theatre,** *Kansas City, Missouri USA*
21 **Orpheum Theatre,** *Memphis, Tennessee USA*
23 **Tennessee Theatre,** *Knoxville, Tennessee USA*
24 **Carpenter Center,** *Richmond, Virginia USA*
25 **Meyerhoff Symphony Hall,** *Baltimore, Maryland USA*
27 **Harrison Opera House,** *Norfolk, Virginia USA*
28 **Thomas Wolfe Auditorium,** *Asheville, North Carolina USA*
29 **Raleigh Memorial Auditorium,** *Raleigh, North Carolina USA*
30 **Blumenthal Performing Arts,** *Charlotte, North Carolina USA*

August
1 **Tupperware Theatre,** *Kissimee, Florida USA*

2 **Kravis Center,** *West Palm Beach, Florida USA*
3 **Tampa Theatre,** *Tampa, Florida USA*
5 **Atlanta Symphony Hall,** *Atlanta, Georgia USA*
6 **Atlanta Symphony Hall,** *Atlanta, Georgia USA*
8 **Ryman Auditorium,** *Nashville, Tennessee USA*
11 **Orpheum Theatre,** *New Orleans, Louisiana USA*
12 **Cullen Performance Hall,** *Houston, Texas USA*
13 **The Backyard,** *Austin, Texas USA*
14 **Majestic Theatre,** *Dallas, Texas USA*
16 **Music Hall,** *Oklahoma City, Oklahoma USA*
18 **Pope Joy Hall,** *Albuquerque, New Mexico USA*
19 **Symphony Hall,** *Phoenix, Arizona USA*
20 **Artemus Ham,** *Las Vegas, Nevada USA*
21 **Symphony Hall,** *San Diego, California USA*
23 **Pantages Theatre,** *Los Angeles, California USA*
24 **Pantages Theatre,** *Los Angeles, California USA*
25 **Pantages Theatre,** *Los Angeles, California USA*
27 **Crawford Hall,** *Irvine, California USA*
28 **Arlington Theatre,** *Santa Barbara, California USA*
30 **Center for Performing Arts,** *San Jose, California USA*
31 **Orpheum Theatre,** *San Francisco, California USA*

September
1 **Orpheum Theatre,** *San Francisco, California USA*
8 **Luther Burbank Center,** *Santa Rosa, California USA*
9 **Sacramento Community Theatre,** *Sacramento, California USA*
10 **Zellerbach Auditorium,** *Berkeley, California USA*
12 **Hult Center,** *Eugene, Oregon USA*
13 **Civic Auditorium,** *Portland, Oregon USA*
14 **Opera House,** *Seattle, Washington USA*
15 **Mt. Baker Theatre,** *Bellingham, Washington USA*
17 **Cottonwood High School,** *Salt Lake City, Utah USA*
19 **Paramount Theatre,** *Denver, Colorado USA*
20 **Mackey Auditorium,** *Boulder, Colorado USA*
22 **Stephens Auditorium,** *Ames, Iowa USA*
23 **Lied Center,** *Lawrence, Kansas USA*
24 **American Theatre,** *St. Louis, Missouri USA*
26 **Egyptian Theatre,** *Dekalb, Illinois USA*
27 **Virginia Theatre,** *Champaign, Illinois USA*
28 **Shryock Auditorium,** *Carbondale, Illinois USA*
29 **Missouri Theatre,** *Columbia, Missouri USA*

October
1 **Pic Staiger,** *Evanston, Illinois USA*
2 **Weidner Center UW,** *Green Bay, Wisconsin USA*
4 **Madison Civic Center,** *Madison, Wisconsin USA*
5 **Riverside Theatre,** *Milwaukee, Wisconsin USA*
7 **Ann Arbor Theatre,** *Ann Arbor, Michigan USA*
8 **Taft Theatre,** *Cincinnati, Ohio USA*
10 **Morris Civic Auditorium,** *South Bend, Indiana USA*
11 **Indiana University,** *Bloomington, Indiana USA*
12 **State Theatre,** *Kalamazoo, Michigan USA*
13 **Masonic Auditorium,** *Toledo, Ohio USA*
15 **Hill Auditorium,** *Ann Arbor, Michigan USA*
16 **Wharton Center,** *East Lansing, Michigan USA*
20 **John M. Green Hall,** *Northhampton, Massachusetts USA*
21 **Maine Center for the Arts,** *Oreno, Maine USA*
22 **Jorgenson Auditorium,** *Storrs, Connecticut USA*
23 **Eisenhower Auditorium,** *University Park, Pennsylvania USA*

25	Clemens Center, *Elmira, New York USA*	23	Nihon Seinenkan Hall, *Tokyo, Japan*
26	Palace Theatre, *New Haven, Connecticut USA*	24	Muse Hall, *Tokyo, Japan*
29	Massey Hall, *Toronto, Ontario Canada*	30	Town Hall, *Auckland, New Zealand*
31	Centennial Hall, *London, Ontario Canada*		

November

December

1	Centre in the Square, *Kitchener, Ontario Canada*	2	Concert Hall, *Melbourne, Australia*
2	Cleary Auditorium, *Windsor, Ontario Canada*	3	Concert Hall, *Melbourne, Australia*
3	National Arts Centre, *Ottawa, Ontario Canada*	4	Concert Hall, *Brisbane, Australia*
5	Hamilton Place, *Hamilton, Ontario Canada*	6	State Theatre, *Sydney, Australia*
6	Grant Hall, *Kingston, Ontario Canada*	7	State Theatre, *Sydney, Australia*
7	Salle Albert-Rosseau, *Ste-Foy, Quebec Canada*	8	State Theatre, *Sydney, Australia*
8	St-Denis Theatre, *Montreal, Quebec Canada*	10	Festival Theatre, *Adelaide, Australia*
22	Club Quattro, *Tokyo, Japan*	12	Concert Hall, *Perth, Australia*
		13	Concert Hall, *Perth, Australia*

1 9 9 6   D E W   D R O P   I N N   T O U R

February

23	Regent Theatre, *Ipswich, England*	16	Tennessee P.A.C., *Nashville, Tennessee USA*
24	City Hall, *Sheffield, England*	17	Orpheum Theater, *Memphis, Tennessee USA*
25	Apollo, *Manchester, England*	19	Palace Theater, *Louisville, Kentucky USA*
27	Usher Hall, *Edinburgh, Scotland*	20	Singletary Center for the Arts, *Lexington, Kentucky USA*
28	Capitol, *Aberdeen, Scotland*		
29	Royal Concert Hall, *Glasgow, Scotland*	21	Thomas Wolfe Auditorium, *Asheville, North Carolina USA*

March

		23	Civic Auditorium, *Knoxville, Tennessee USA*
1	City Hall, *Hull, England*	24	The Township, *Columbia, South Carolina USA*
3	Royal Centre, *Nottingham, England*	26	Constitution Hall, *Washington DC USA*
4	Philharmonic, *Liverpool, England*	27	Constitution Hall, *Washington DC USA*
5	City Hall, *Newcastle, England*	28	Constitution Hall, *Washington DC USA*
6	Civic Hall, *Wolverhampton, England*		
8	Royal Albert Hall, *London, England*	May	
9	Royal Albert Hall, *London, England*	1	Tower Theater, *Philadelphia, Pennsylvania USA*
11	Exeter University, *Exeter, England*	2	Tower Theater, *Philadelphia, Pennsylvania USA*
12	Colston Hall, *Bristol, England*	3	Tower Theater, *Philadelphia, Pennsylvania USA*
13	Guildhall, *Portsmouth, England*	5	St. Denis, *Montreal, Quebec Canada*
15	Congresbouw, *Den Haag, Holland*	6	St. Denis, *Montreal, Quebec Canada*
16	RAI Congrescentrum, *Amsterdam, Holland*	7	Auditorium, *Burlington, Vermont USA*
18	Grand Rex, *Paris, France*	8	UNH Arena, *Durham, New Hampshire USA*
19	Phillipshalle, *Dusseldorf, Germany*	10	Palace Theater, *Albany, New York USA*
20	CCH Saal 1, *Hamburg, Germany*	11	Palace, *New Haven, Connecticut USA*
21	The Forest National, *Brussels, Belgium*	13	The Paramount, *New York City USA*
22	Beethovenshalle, *Stuttgart, Germany*	14	The Paramount, *New York City USA*
24	Alte Opera, *Frankfurt, Germany*	15	The Paramount, *New York City USA*
25	Friedrichstadt Palast, *Berlin, Germany*	17	Symphony Hall, *Springfield, Massachusetts USA*
26	Philharmonie, *Munich, Germany*	18	Landmark Theatre, *Syracuse, New York USA*
28	Teatro Tenda, *Florence, Italy*	19	Kirby Center, *Wilkes-Barre, Pennsylvania USA*
29	Teatro Nazionale, *Milan, Italy*	21	Wang Center, *Boston, Massachusetts USA*
		22	Wang Center, *Boston, Massachusetts USA*
April		25	Shea's Performing Arts Center, *Buffalo, New York USA*
9	Tampa Bay P.A.C., *Tampa, Florida USA*		
10	Performing Arts Center, *Gainesville, Florida USA*	26	Alumni Hall, *London, Ontario Canada*
12	Sunrise Musical Theatre, *Fort Lauderdale, Florida USA*	27	Massey Hall, *Toronto, Ontario Canada*
13	University of Central Florida Arena, *Orlando, Florida USA*	28	Massey Hall, *Toronto, Ontario Canada*
		30	Benedum Center, *Pittsburgh, Pennsylvania USA*
14	Fox Theater, *Atlanta, Georgia USA*	31	Fox Theatre, *Detroit, Michigan USA*

June

2	**Welsh Auditorium,** *Grand Rapids, Michigan USA*		16	**Paramount,** *Seattle, Washington USA*
3	**Aranoff Center,** *Cincinnati, Ohio USA*		17	**Paramount,** *Seattle, Washington USA*
4	**Music Hall,** *Cleveland, Ohio USA*		19	**Orpheum Theatre,** *Vancouver, British Columbia Canada*
6	**Rosemont Theatre,** *Chicago, Illinois USA*		20	**Hult Center,** *Eugene, Oregon USA*
7	**Rosemont Theatre,** *Chicago, Illinois USA*		21	**Schnitzer Auditorium,** *Portland, Oregon USA*
8	**Riverside Theatre,** *Milwaukee, Wisconsin USA*		23	**Morrison PAC,** *Boise, Idaho USA*
10	**Northrup Auditorium,** *Minneapolis, Minnesota USA*		26	**Paramount,** *Cedar Rapids, Iowa USA*
11	**CY Stephens Auditorium,** *Arnes, Iowa USA*		27	**Sagamon State University Auditorium,** *Springfield, Illinois USA*
12	**TBA,** *St. Louis, Missouri USA*			
13	**Memorial Hall,** *Kansas City, Kansas USA*		28	**Murat Theatre,** *Indianapolis, Indiana USA*
15	**Bronco Bowl,** *Dallas, Texas USA*		29	**Peoria Civic Theatre,** *Peoria, Illinois USA*
16	**The Backyard,** *Austin, Texas USA*		31	**Stranahan,** *Toledo, Ohio USA*
17	**Cullen Auditorium,** *Houston, Texas USA*			
19	**Paramount Theatre,** *Denver, Colorado USA*		August	
20	**Paramount Theatre,** *Denver, Colorado USA*		1	**Palace Theatre,** *Columbus, Ohio USA*
21	**Abravenal Hall,** *Salt Lake City, Utah USA*		2	**Memorial Auditorium,** *Dayton, Ohio USA*
23	**County Bowl,** *Santa Barbara, California USA*		4	**Tivoli Theatre,** *Chatanooga, Tennessee USA*
24	**Aladdin Theater,** *Las Vegas, Nevada USA*		5	**Alabama Theatre,** *Birmingham, Alabama USA*
25	**Civic Theater,** *San Diego, California USA*		7	**Thaila Mara Hall,** *Jackson, Mississippi USA*
28	**The Greek,** *Los Angeles, California USA*		8	**Chastain Park Amphitheatre,** *Atlanta, Georgia USA*
29	**The Greek,** *Los Angeles, California USA*		10	**Bayfront Auditorium,** *Pensacola, Florida USA*
30	**The Greek,** *Los Angeles, California USA*		11	**Florida Theatre,** *Jacksonville, Florida USA*
			14	**Galliard Municipal Auditorium,** *Charleston, South Carolina USA*
July				
2	**Symphony Hall,** *Phoenix, Arizona USA*		15	**Raleigh Memorial Auditorium,** *Raleigh, North Carolina USA*
10	**Community Theatre,** *Sacramento, California USA*			
11	**Paramount Theatre,** *Oakland, California USA*		16	**Wolf Trap,** *Vienna, Virginia USA*
12	**Paramount Theatre,** *Oakland, California USA*		25	**Jones Beach Theatre,** *Wantaugh, New York USA*
14	**SJ State Events Center,** *San Jose, California USA*		26	**Garden State Arts Center,** *Holmdel, New Jersey USA*

DISCOGRAPHY

ELLEN AMOS

Baltimore / Walking With You
7"; MEA 5290 (private pressing 1980)

Y KANT TORI READ

Singles

The Big Picture / You Go To My Head
7"; Atlantic 89086 (June 1988)
Cool On Your Island / Heart Attack at 23
7"; Atlantic 89021 (August 1988)

Album

Y Kant Tori Read
The Big Picture / Cool On Your Island / Fayth / Fire On The Side / Pirates / Floating City / Heart Attack at 23 / On The Boundary / You Go To My Head / Etienne Trilogy (The Highland, Etienne, Skyeboat Song)
CD, LP, Cassette; Atlantic 81845 (1988)

Promotional Singles

The Big Picture / The Big Picture
7"; Atlantic 89086 and 12"; Atlantic PR2298 (June 1988)
Cool On Your Island (edit) / Cool On Your Island (edit)
7"; Atlantic 89021 (August 1988)
Cool On Your Island
Cool On Your Island (edit) / Cool On Your Island (LP version) / Phil Collins: A Groovy Kind Of Love
CD; Atlantic PR2452 (1988)

TORI AMOS

U.S.A. Singles/EPs

Silent All These Years / Upside Down
Cassette; Atlantic 87511 (1992)
Crucify
Crucify (remix) / Winter / Angie (Jagger/Richards) / Smells Like Teen Spirit (Cobain/Nirvana) / Thank You (Plant/Page)
CD, Cassette; Atlantic 82399-2 (May 1992)
Crucify (Remix) / Me and a Gun
Cassette; Atlantic 87463 (1992)
Winter
Winter / The Pool / Take To The Sky / Sweet Dreams / Upside Down
Limited Edition CD; Atlantic 85799 (November 1992)

Winter (edit) / The Pool
Cassette; Atlantic 87418 (November 1992)
God
God / Home On The Range (Cherokee Edition) / Piano Suite: All The Girls Hate Her, Over It
CD; Atlantic 85687-2 (February 1994)
Cornflake Girl
Cornflake Girl (edit) / Sister Janet / Daisy Dead Petals / Honey
CD; Atlantic 85655-2 (April 1994)
Caught a Lite Sneeze
Caught a Lite Sneeze / Silly Songs: This Old Man / That's What I Like Mick (The Sandwich Song) / Graveyard / Toodles Mr. Jim
CD; Atlantic 85519-2

U.K. Singles/EPs

Me And A Gun
Silent All These Years / Upside Down / Me And A Gun / Thoughts
Picture Disc CD, 12"; East West YZ618 (October 1991)
Silent All These Years
Reissue of *Me And A Gun* CD as above
Picture Disc CD; East West YZ618 (November 1991)
China / Sugar
Cassette, 7"; East West A7531 (January 1992)
China
China / Sugar / Flying Dutchman / Humpty Dumpty
CD, 12"; East West A7531 (January 1992)
Winter / The Pool
Cassette, 7"; East West A7504 (March 1992)
Winter
Winter / The Pool / Take To The Sky / Sweet Dreams
CD; East West A7504 (March 1992)
Winter
Winter / Angie (Jagger/Richards) / Smells Like Teen Spirit (Cobain/Nirvana) / Thank You (Plant/Page)
Limited Edition CD; East West A7504 (March 1992)
Crucify (remix) / Here. in my head
Cassette, 7"; East West A7479 (June 1992)
Crucify
Crucify (remix) / Here. In My Head / Mary / Crucify (LP version)
CD; East West A7479 (June 1992)
Crucify
Little Earthquakes (Live) / Crucify (Live) / Precious Things (Live) / Mother (Live)
Limited Edition CD Box containing four miniature art prints;
East West A7479 (June 1992)
Silent All These Years / Me and a Gun
Cassette; East West YZ618C

Silent All These Years
Silent All These Years / Smells Like Teen Spirit (Cobain/Nirvana)
Cassette, 7"; East West A7433 (August 1992)
Silent All These Years
Silent All These Years / Upside Down / Me And A Gun / Thoughts
CD; East West A7433 (August 1992)
Silent All These Years
Silent All These Years / Ode To The Banana King (Part One) / Song For Eric / Happy Phantom (Live)
Limited Edition CD; East West A7433 (August 1992)
Cornflake Girl / Sister Janet
Cassette, 7"; East West A7281 (January 1994)
Cornflake Girl
Cornflake Girl / Sister Janet / Piano Suite: All The Girls Hate Her, Over It
CD; East West A7281 (January 10, 1994)
Cornflake Girl
Cornflake Girl / A Case Of You (Joni Mitchell) / If 6 Was 9 (Jimi Hendrix) / Strange Fruit (L. Allan)
Limited Edition CD; East West A7281 (January 17, 1994)
Pretty Good Year / Honey
Cassette, 7"; East West A7263 (March 1994)
Pretty Good Year - Disc 1
Pretty Good Year / Home On The Range with Cherokee addition [sic] / Daisy Dead Petals
Limited Edition CD; East West A7263 (March 1994)
Pretty Good Year - Disc 2
Pretty Good Year / Honey / Black Swan
CD; East West A7263 (March 1994)
Past The Mission (LP version) / Past The Mission (Live)
Cassette, 7"; East West A7257 (May 1994)
Past The Mission - Disc 1
Upside Down (Live) / Past The Mission (Live) / Icicle (Live) / Flying Dutchman (Live)
CD; East West A7257 (May 1994)
Past The Mission - Disc 2
Past The Mission / Winter (Live) / The Waitress (Live) / Here. in my Head (Live)
CD; East West A7257 (May 1994)
Caught a Lite Sneeze
Caught a Lite Sneeze / Silly Songs: This Old Man / Hungarian Wedding Song / Toodles Mr. Jim
CD; East West A5524CD1
Caught a Lite Sneeze
Caught a Lite Sneeze Tribute to Chas and Dave: London Girls / That's What I Like Mick (The Sandwich Song) / Samurai
CD; East West A5524CD2

Talula
Talula (the tornado mix) / Frog On My Toe / Sister Named Desire / Alamo
CD; East West A8512CD2 7567-88511-2 (March 1996)
Talula
Talula (the tornado mix) / Talula (BT's synethasia mix) / Amazing Grace/Til The Chicken
CD; East West A8512CD1 7567-88512-2 (March 1996)

French Singles/EPs

Crucify / Here. in my head
CD; East West 87479 (1992)
Crucify
Crucify / Angie (Jagger/Richards) / Smells Like Teen Spirit (Cobain/Nirvana)
CD; East West/WEA 85787 (1992)

German Singles/EPs

Me And A Gun
Silent All These Years / Upside Down / Me And A Gun / Thoughts
CD; East West YZ618 (October 1991)
Winter
Winter / Smells Like Teen Spirit (Cobain/Nirvana) / Angie (Jagger/Richards)
Cassette; WEA 85862-4 (1992)
Winter
Winter / The Pool / Smells Like Teen Spirit (Cobain/Nirvana)
CD; East West LC 1557 (1992)
Silent All These Years
Silent All These Years / Smells Like Teen Spirit (Cobain/Nirvana)
7"; East West 76013 (1992)

Japanese Singles/EPs

Silent All These Years / Me And A Gun
3" CD; East West WMD5-4102 (April 1992)

New Zealand Singles/EPs

Pretty Good Year
Pretty Good Year / Honey / Black Swan
CD; East West A7263 (March 1994)

Albums

Little Earthquakes
Crucify / Girl / Silent All These Years / Precious Things / Winter / Happy Phantom / China / Leather / Mother / Tear In Your Hand / Me And A Gun / Little Earthquakes
UK: CD, LP, Cassette; East West 7567-82358 (January 1992)
USA: CD, Cassette; Atlantic 82358 (February 1992) and Mini Disc; Atlantic 7-82358 (1993)
Japan: CD; WEA WMC5-438 (April 1992)

Under The Pink
Pretty Good Year / God / Bells For Her / Past the Mission / Baker Baker / The Wrong Band / The Waitress / Cornflake Girl / Icicle / Cloud On My Tongue / Space Dog / Yes, Anastasia
UK: CD, LP, Cassette; East West 7567-82567 (January 1994)
USA: CD, Cassette; Atlantic 82567 (February 1994)
Japan: CD; WEA AMCE-553 (February 1994)

Boys for Pele
Beauty Queen / Horses / Blood Roses / Father Lucifer / Professional Widow / Mr Zebra / Marianne / Cauth a Lite Sneeze / Muhammad My Friend / Hey Jupiter / Way Down / Little Amsterdam / Talula / Not The Red Baron / Agent Orange / Doughnut Song / In The Springtime of His Voodoo / Putting The Damage On / Twinkle
USA: CD, Cassette; Atlantic 82862-2 (February 1996)

Guest Appearances

Al Stewart: Last Days of the Century
backing vocals: Last Day of the Century / Red Toupee
CD, LP, Cassette; Enigma 73316 (1988)

Stan Ridgeway: Mosquitos
backing vocals: Dogs / Peg and Pete and Me / The Last Honest Man
CD, LP, Cassette; Geffen 2-24216 (1989)

Sandra Bernhard: Without You I'm Nothing
backing vocals: Little Red Corvette (Prince)
CD, LP, Cassette; Enigma 73369 CD (1989)

Ferron: Phantom Center
backing vocals
CD, Cassette; Chameleon 4-74830 (1990)

Toys - Music from the Original Motion Picture Soundtrack
The Happy Worker / Workers
CD, Cassette; Geffen 24505 (1992)

Ruby Trax
Ring My Bell (Knight)
CD, LP Box Set; Forty Records NME40CD (1992)

Kevin and Bean: We've Got Your Yule Logs Hangin'
Little Drummer Boy (Live) (Traditional)
Cassette; KROQCS-4 KROQ Radio charity cassette (1992)

Speaking of Christmas and Other Things
Spoken word with accompaniment: Sarah Sylvia Cynthia Stout Would Not Take The Garbage Out (Shel Silverstein)
Cassette; KZON Radio charity cassette (1992)

Promotional Albums

Little Earthquakes
same track listing as released version
Cassette; Atlantic 82358-4A (1991) issued with black & white promo only cover

Under The Pink
Same track listing as released version
CD; Atlantic 5398-2 (December 1993) gatefold digipak w/ unapproved cover photo destroyed; white CD shipped in clear jewel box
Cassette; Atlantic 5397-4 82567-4 (December 1993) majority of cassette covers also destroyed; some shipped

Boys for Pele
same track listing as released version
Cassette; Atlantic 82862-4 (1996) issued with black & white promo only cover

Promotional Singles

Silent All These Years
CD; Atlantic PR4454-2 (1992)

Crucify (remix)
CD; Atlantic PR4598 (1992)

Precious Things
Precious Things / Mother (Live) / Upside Down / Mary / Flying Dutchman
Picture Disc CD; Atlantic PR4742-2 (1992)

Winter (edit) / Winter
CD; Atlantic PR4800 (1992)

Little Drummer Boy (Live)
CD; Atlantic PR5409 (December 1993)

Cornflake Girl
Cornflake Girl (edit) / Sister Janet / Piano Suite: All The Girls Hate Her, Over It
CD; East West A7281CDDJ (December 1993)

God
God / Home On The Range (Cherokee Edition) / The Waitress
CD; Atlantic PR5408-2 (January 1994)

God
CD; Atlantic PR5398-2 (January 1994)

Tea With The Waitress
Part 1: Interview with Bob Waugh of WHFS-FM interspersed with samples of songs from *Under The Pink*.
Part 2: Tori's answers only from the interview
CD; Atlantic PR5498-2 (March 1994)

God
God (no guitar) / God (some guitar) / God (LP version)
CD; Atlantic PR5573 (March 1994)

Caught a Lite Sneeze
Caught a Lite Sneeze / Hey Jupiter / Talula / Putting the Damage On
Cassette; Atlantic PRCS6608 (1996)

Videos

Little Earthquakes
Silent All These Years (Video) / Leather (Live) / Precious Things (Live) / Crucify (Video) / Me And A Gun (Live

TV appearance) / Little Earthquakes (Live) / China (Video) / Happy Phantom (Live) / Here. in my head (Live) / Winter (Video) / Song for Eric (Live)
A*Vision Entertainment 50335-3 (1992)

Music Folios

Little Earthquakes
Crucify / Girl / Silent All These Years / Precious Things / Winter / Happy Phantom / China / Leather / Mother / Tear In Your Hand / Me And A Gun / Little Earthquakes / Upside Down / Thoughts
Amsco Publications AM90041 US ISBN 0.8256.1345.0 UK ISBN 0.7119.3117.8

Under The Pink
Pretty Good Year / God / Bells for Her / Past the Mission / Baker Baker / The Wrong Band / The Waitress / Cornflake Girl / Icicle / Cloud on my Tongue / Space Dog / Yes, Anastasia / All The Girls Hate Her / Over It
Amsco Publications AM92048 US ISBN 0.8256.1405.8 UK ISBN 0.7119.4178.5

The Bee Sides
Baltimore / Black Swan / Butterfly / Daisy Dead Petals / Etienne / Floating City / Flying Dutchman / Here. In My Head / Home on the Range: Cherokee Edition / Honey / Humpty Dumpty / Mary / Ode To The Banana King (Part 1) / Sister Janet / Song For Eric / Sugar / Sweet Dreams / Take To The Sky
Amsco Publications AM 931315 UK ISBN 0.8256.1494.5 UK ISBN 0.7119.5132.2

Boys for Pele
Beauty Queen / Horses / Blood Roses / Father Lucifer / Professional Widow / Mr Zebra / Marianne / Cauth a Lite Sneeze / Muhammad My Friend / Hey Jupiter / Way Down / Little Amsterdam / Talula / Not The Red Baron / Agent Orange / Doughnut Song / In The Springtime of His Voodoo / Putting The Damage On / Twinkle
Amsco Publications AM 937750 UK ISBN 0.8256.1544.5 UK ISBN 0.7119.5794.0

Fan Clubs

Upside Down, Tori Amos Fan Club
Contact: Tom Richards
PO Box 8456
Clearwater, FL 34618 USA
Fax: (813) 461-2922

Really Deep Thoughts Fanzine
Contact: Melissa and Richard Caldwell
PO Box 328606
Columbus, OH 43232 USA
Newsline: (614) 792-8836

Take To The Sky Fanzine
Contact: Steve Jenkins
25 Rydall Drive
Bexleyheath, Kent DA7 5EF England

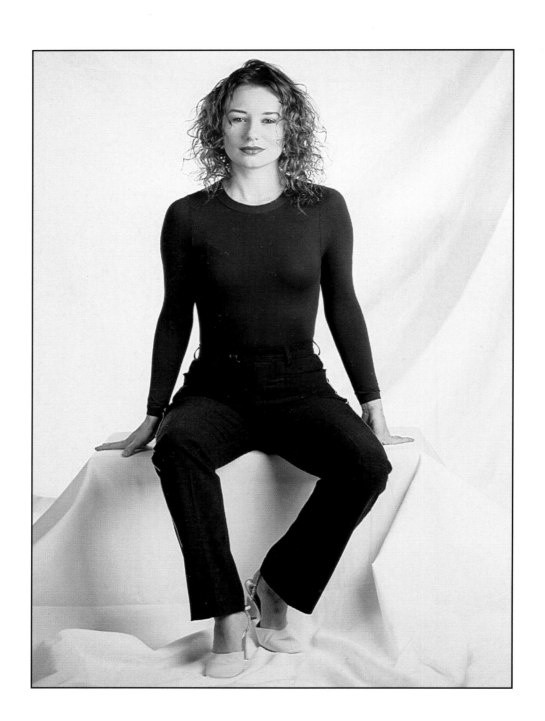